THE
HAYLING RAILWAY

by
Peter Paye

THE OAKWOOD PRESS

© Oakwood Press & Peter Paye 2013

First edition published 1979
Second revised edition published 2013

British Library Cataloguing in Publication Data
A Record for this book is available from the British Library
ISBN 978 0 85361 730 3

Typeset by Oakwood Graphics.
Repro by PKmediaworks, Cranborne, Dorset.
Printed by Gomer Press, Llandysul, Ceredigion.

The late afternoon sun casts long shadows over Hayling Island station and goods yard in November 1962, as 'A1X' 0-6-0 No. No 32650 waits to depart for Havant with her two-coach train in the main platform road. *Author*

Title page: High tide at Langstone Harbour as the 12.55 pm Hayling Island to Havant train hauled by diminutive 'A1X' class 0-6-0T No. 32650 negotiates the timbers of Langston bridge in November 1962. Langston Bridge signal box is to the left (just visible). *Author*

Front cover: The sun sets over the Hayling Railway. 'A1X' class 0-6-0T No. 32650 hauls its branch passenger train over Langston bridge on 2nd November, 1963, the last day of public service. *Roy Hobbs*

Rear cover: The route of the Hayling Island branch reproduced to scale from the 1 inch scale Ordnance Survey map, No. 181 Chichester, of 1947. The Hayling branch can be seen heading due south from Havant. The main line through Havant to the west is to Portsmouth and Fareham, and to the east, to Chichester and Brighton. The railway heading due north from Havant is to Petersfield and Guildford. *Crown Copyright*

Published by The Oakwood Press (Usk), P.O. Box 13, Usk, Mon., NP15 1YS.
E-mail: sales@oakwoodpress.co.uk
Website: www.oakwoodpress.co.uk

Contents

With safety valves lifting 'Terrier' class 0-6-0T No 32650 heads a Havant to Hayling Island branch train across the 1,100 ft-long Langston bridge at high tide on 29th October, 1962.

Ken Paye

Activity at the north end of South Hayling platform showing 'A1' class 0-6-0T No 78 *Knowle* waiting to depart. This view is interesting for its shows the engine shed in the background and the only just visible primitive down home and up starting signal arms mounted on the same post. *Roger Nash Collection*

Langston level crossing No. 4 at 1 mile 07 chains from Havant was a constant thorn in the flesh of road users travelling from the mainland to and from Hayling Island and on post-war summer Saturdays the traffic lined up for miles each side of the gates. Here at a quieter time 'A1X' class 0-6-0T No. 32650 approaches Langston with the 2.20 pm from Havant in November 1962. The gatekeeper is placing the down signal to danger in the six-lever ground frame on the left before opening the gates after the train had cleared the crossing. *Author*

Introduction

A gentle sea breeze cools the heat of an August summer Saturday, gulls wheel in the azure blue sky and shore birds rummage for food on the mudflats, as yachtsmen take advantage of any wind available to negotiate their vessels within the confines of Langstone Harbour. Two bridges, one road and the other rail, span the sparkling water of the haven, both connecting mainland Hampshire with the island of Hayling situated east of Portsmouth and within view of the Isle of Wight across the Solent. The tranquil scene is shattered by the blast of an engine whistle as a small 0-6-0 tank locomotive, with tall chimney, hauling five relatively elderly coaches negotiates the timber viaduct and rumbles over the iron central swing section, the train en route from the junction at Havant to Hayling Island. The procession rumbles effortlessly on to its destination and soon the sound of the train diminishes and calm returns. The scene will be repeated four times every hour, two trains heading to the coast bearing expectant parents with their luggage and children with buckets and spades looking forward to a day by the sea or their annual holiday, whilst those trains returning north convey crowds complete with cases, 'kiss me quick' hats and the like, who will have happy memories of time spent in hotels, boarding houses, holiday camps and on the beach.

The location remains but the scene changes to a bitterly cold winter's day, snow is threatening and the sky is a dull forbidding grey. Gulls still wheel in the air but few shore birds forage, and there is precious little sight of any movement on the water save for the wind across the surface. Again a whistle is heard and again the diminutive locomotive, leaking steam in the cold air makes for the bridge but this time all she has in tow is a solitary brake/composite coach bearing few passengers. The service is sparse and the observer might have to wait for more than an hour before the return working.

Such scenes register the two extremes of passenger traffic handled on the Havant to Hayling Island branch where many thousands of passengers were conveyed during the summer months and comparatively few in the winter. The line was famous for the fact that, except in the early years, the London, Brighton & South Coast Railway (LBSCR), Southern Railway (SR) and British Railways Southern Region operated the line with Stroudley-designed 'A', then 'A1' and later as rebuilt 'A1X' class 'Terrier' 0-6-0 tank locomotives necessitated by the weight restrictions imposed by the respective civil engineers on Langston viaduct, ensuring a place in the annals of railway history. The combination of the infamous Beeching Report, the deteriorating condition of the viaduct and the ageing locomotives brought closure of the branch on and from 4th November, 1963, the last train running the previous day.

The publication of this book coincides with the 50th anniversary of the closure of the erstwhile Hayling Railway (HR) linking Havant in East Hampshire with Hayling Island. Before the coming of the railway Hayling Island, located immediately east of the more famous and illustrious island of Portsea on which stands Portsmouth, the world famous and renowned naval port, was sparsely populated by fishermen, agricultural workers and gentry who had established residences near the south coast of the island. After the opening of the LBSCR main line from Brighton to Havant on 15th March, 1847, extended to Portsmouth on 14th June, 1847, and the later 'Portsmouth Direct' connection on 1st January, 1859 operated by the London & South Western Railway (LSWR), local factions pressed for a rail connection to the island from Havant using the route of a goods line to Langstone Harbour, authorized in 1851 but never built. An 1860 Act of Parliament authorized such a route with a bridge across Langstone Harbour and thence as an inspired economy measure to run along a causeway on the western side of the island, removing the expensive necessity of purchasing land. It was anticipated that the enclosed waters of Langstone Harbour would obviate problems with tidal erosion but this assumption proved incorrect and a second Act of 1864 authorized a new alignment on terra firma just above high water mark. The purpose of the railway was not to serve the scattered communities but develop holiday traffic to the west town district where a hotel and partly completed crescent had been constructed as well as provision of docks to encourage freight traffic to the new line.

After many trials and tribulations the new railway opened in 1867 with train services initially operated by the contractor. The Act authorizing the construction of the overland route and abandonment of the ambitious docks scheme unusually received the Royal Assent 26 days after the railway opened for traffic! Severe weather and the erosion of the trackbed near North Hayling resulted in closure of the line for several months and the piecemeal operation of the railway finally came to a conclusion on 1st January, 1872 when the Hayling Railway was leased to the LBSCR at a guaranteed rent of £2,000 per annum, the HR remaining nominally independent until absorbed by the company in November 1922. The new operator set about making important changes, including an ill-fated train ferry service operating between Langstone Quay and St Helen's to join up with the Isle of Wight Railway from 1882 until 1888. Around the turn of the century improvements were made at South Hayling, renamed Hayling Island from June 1892, but to all intents and purposes the railway was operated as one of the many LBSCR minor branch lines. As a result of the 1921 Railways Act the erstwhile Hayling Railway became part of the Southern Railway from 1st January, 1923 and the new regime carried out substantial work on Langston viaduct, the major infrastructure on the branch, completed in 1931, and the reconstruction of Havant station in 1937/38. Development in the locality was sparse and substantial growth was not achieved until the late 1920s and 1930s, and then primarily near the south and south-eastern corner of the island. The establishment of holiday camps both before and after World War II and paid holidays encouraged many to the coast and increased passenger traffic receipts especially during the summer months. The line entered nationalization from 1st January, 1948 but initially few changes were made and, except for an improvement in coaching stock and wagons, motive power remained the same.

As the years progressed it became obvious that the timber viaduct required substantial remedial work after decades of exposure to the elements; modernization was the watchword on British Railways (BR) and the ancient 'Terrier' 0-6-0 tank locomotives were increasingly costly to maintain. Revenue, except during the summer months although still covering operating costs, was declining. The rebuilding of the parallel road bridge to the island in 1956 allowing increased weight limit for vehicles, especially buses, and the later abolition of tolls for road traffic in 1960 weighed heavily against retention of the branch railway, which proved an expensive luxury that the cost-conscious BR could ill afford. Closure of the line, originally mooted in the 1950s was resurrected in 1962 and confirmed in the infamous Beeching Report of 1963 that closure was already under consideration. By then steps were well advanced and after the obligatory Transport Users' Consultative Committee (TUCC) hearing, objections to closure were overruled and the Minister of Transport authorized BR to effect complete closure on and from Monday 4th November, 1963, the last public trains running on 2nd November and a special train on Sunday 3rd November.

This then is the fascinating story of the Hayling Railway from conception to closure. I have attempted to trace the history of the line and details have been checked with available documents, but apologies are offered for any errors, which might have occurred.

Note: The spelling of Langston as used by the LBSCR from May 1873 has been used throughout the text for railway reference but Langstone for geographical purposes.

Chapter One

Advent of the Railway

Havant, a small market town with a population in 1961 of 32,450, is situated in the south-east corner of the county of Hampshire overlooking Langstone Harbour. For many years it was a manufacturing centre for the leather and parchment industries with sheepskins hanging in the streets to dry. Roman invaders landed near the site of the town to stay in the area for over 400 years, but local volunteer defence groups thwarted later Napoleonic landings.

To the south of Havant and opposite Langstone is Hayling Island, some four miles long and with an area of 10 square miles. It has for its close western neighbour the Island of Portsea, on which stands the City of Portsmouth and the seaside resort of Southsea. To the east are Chichester Harbour and Selsey. Hayling has for more than two centuries enjoyed the reputation as a watering place and seaside resort. The natural surroundings and amenities make it ideal for family holidays without overpowering commercial attractions, and sailing and boating are popular in the sheltered waters of Langstone Harbour. Much of the northern area of Hayling Island is rich farming land, and development was sparse and fragmentary with substantial growth only occurring near the south and south-eastern corner of the island from the late 1920s. Post-war development included the provision of three large holiday camps catering for many thousands of visitors. The advent of the railway between Havant and Hayling Island, initially to engender trade at Langstone, was also of prime importance in the development of increasing holiday trade to the island.

The first permanent access to Hayling from the mainland, to relieve the island from its status as an isolated manorial parish, was a single-lane wooden road bridge, 860 ft in length, connecting Langstone with the north shore and built in 1823 and 1824 by Sir George Thomas Staunton, who was Lord of the Manor of Havant. The only other access was by ferry at the western extremity of the island, privately owned and providing a link with Portsea Island and Portsmouth, a forerunner of today's municipal ferry. The Parliamentary powers for 'Building a Bridge and making a Causeway from Langstone in the Parish of Havant, in the County of Southampton to Hayling Island in the Parish of North Hayling, in the said County, at or near a certain house there, called the Ferry House; and for forming and making proper roads or avenues thereto', were obtained by the Duke of Norfolk on 2nd May, 1823 (4 Geo. 4 cap. ix). The statute authorized The Company of Proprietors of the Hayling Bridge and Causeway to raise £12,000 for the work, with borrowing powers for a further £4,000 later. As well as building the bridge and causeway the company was also to provide:

> … proper and convenient Docks, Wharfs, Quays or Landingplaces [*sic*] on either side of the said harbour, adjoining or near the said Bridge or Causeway, for the shipping and landing of Goods, Wares, Merchandise and other things into and out of ships, barges and other vessels navigating or using the said harbour, and also to erect one or more Warehouse or Warehouses, Weighbeams and Cranes for receiving, weighing and landing the said Goods, Wares and Merchandise.

The Manorial rights of Hayling and ownership of the bridge were subsequently sold to William Padwick. As a result of the Act the company constructed a dock on the eastern side of the bridge and a wharf, with berthing for vessels on the western side of the structure.

ANNO DECIMO QUARTO & DECIMO QUINTO

VICTORIÆ REGINÆ.

****

Cap. lxviii.

An Act to enable the Company of Proprietors of the *Hayling Bridge* and Causeway to construct a Railway from their Docks and Wharves at *Langstone* to join the *London, Brighton, and South Coast* Railway at *Havant* in the County of Southampton.   [*3d July* 1851.]

WHEREAS by an Act passed in the Fourth Year of the Reign of His Majesty King *George* the Fourth, intituled *An Act for building a Bridge and making a Causeway* 4 G. 4 *from* Langstone *in the Parish of* Havant *in the County of* South-ampton *to* Hayling Island *in the Parish of* Hayling North *in the said County, at or near a certain House there called the* Ferry House, *and for forming and making proper Roads, Approaches, and Avenues thereto,* a Company were incorporated by the Name of " The Company of Proprietors of the *Hayling Bridge* and Cause-way," and such Company have constructed the Bridge and Causeway by such Act authorized to be made : And whereas by such Act the Company are authorized to construct proper and convenient Docks, Wharves, Quays, or Landing Places on either Side of *Langstone* Harbour, adjoining or near the said Bridge and Causeway, for the

[*Local.*]   11 *O*   shipping

Hayling Bridge and Causeway Act, 3rd July, 1851 authorizing the company to connect a railway from the wharves and docks at Langstone to the LBSCR at Havant.

With the opening of the London Brighton & South Coast Railway west coast route from Brighton to Portsmouth via Chichester to Havant on 15th March, 1847 and extended to Portsmouth on 14th June of that year, the Hayling Bridge and Causeway Company considered it necessary to form a connection at Havant. The Hayling Bridge and Causeway (Railway to Havant) Act of 3rd July, 1851 (14 and 15 Vict. cap lxviii), duly authorized the company,

> … to construct a railway commencing from or near such Bridge and Causeway at or near the Toll House situated in the Parish of Havant and terminating at or near a point on the said LBSCR, where the said railway crosses a lane called New Lane in the Parishes of Havant and Warblington, or one of them, in the County of Southampton.

Clause V authorized the provision of level crossings over public roads Nos. 5, 52 and 54 in the Parish of Havant, Turnpike Road No. 21 in the parish of Havant and Turnpike Road No. 11 in the parish of Warblington.

Clause vi forced the use of horse traction for it stipulated, 'That the Company shall not use the Railway with Carriages propelled by steam or by Atmospheric Agency, or drawn by ropes in connection with a stationary steam engine; and if the Company use the said railway with carriages drawn or propelled as aforesaid, they shall forfeit for every said offence the sum of Twenty Pounds'. The junction with the LBSCR at Havant was to be made under the direction and to the satisfaction of the LBSCR Engineer. Two years were allowed for the compulsory purchase of land and three years for the completion of works. The 1823 Act authorized the creation of £12,000 shares, but only £9,500 had been raised and the balancing number of shares had been forfeited. The new statute authorized the raising of £3,000 by mortgage or bonds in lieu of the original £4,000 borrowing powers and sanctioned the company to raise new capital of £5,000.

Soon after the passing of the Act plans were proposed for the provision of commercial and dry docks in the Portsmouth and Langstone area to improve facilities for the import and export of goods round the world and possibly obviating shipping having to sail through the Straits of Dover and up the Thames to the Port of London. The vulnerability of merchants' shipping would thus be safeguarded by the presence of the Royal Navy at Portsmouth and the existence of Cumberland Fort on the Portsmouth side of Langstone Harbour and a Martello tower on the Hayling side. The *Naval Chronicle* of 1855 recorded that the Admiralty had consented to the construction of an embankment from the proposed railway bridge to the harbour entrance on the Hayling Island side of Langstone Harbour. The channel from the harbour entrance to Langstone Quay was to be considerably deepened and widened to aid the passage of vessels. A railway line running along the embankment was proposed leading to the harbour entrance where wet, dry and timber docks were to be built together with warehousing and discharge facilities abreast of Sinah Lake. Two years were allowed for the completion of the railway but no time was given for completion of the dock facilities. Nothing came of the venture possibly because of the road bridge connecting the mainland and Hayling Island, the constant silting up of Langstone Harbour and more importantly the inability of the Hayling Bridge and Causeway Co. to raise sufficient capital which resulted in the powers granted in the 1851 Act to lapse.

On 1st January, 1859 the Direct Portsmouth Railway from Godalming, acquired by the London & South Western Railway, opened its Portsmouth direct line to Havant, amidst violent protest from the LBSCR, and brought London within 66

ANNO VICESIMO TERTIO & VICESIMO QUARTO

VICTORIÆ REGINÆ.

✱✱✱

Cap. clxvi.

An Act for making Railways between the *London, Brighton, and South Coast* and *Direct Portsmouth* Railways and *Hayling Ferry,* and for other Purposes. [23d *July* 1860.]

WHEREAS the making and maintaining of Railways between the *London, Brighton, and South Coast* and the *Direct Portsmouth* Railways in the Parish of *Havant* and *Hayling Ferry* would be of great public Advantage : And whereas Plans and Sections of the intended Railways and other Works showing the Lines and Levels thereof, and also a Book of Reference containing the Names of the Owners or reputed Owners, Lessees or reputed Lessees, and Occupiers of the Land through or upon which the same is intended to pass, be made, or which may be required for the Purpose of the Undertaking, have been deposited with the Clerk of the Peace of the County of *Southampton* : And whereas the Persons herein-after named, with other Persons and Corporations, are willing, at their own Expense, to carry the said Undertaking into execution, if authorized by Parliament so to do : May it therefore please Your Majesty that it be enacted : and be it enacted by the Queen's most Excellent Majesty, by and with the Advice and Consent of the Lords Spiritual and Temporal, and Commons, in this present Parlia-

[*Local.*]   27 N   ment

miles of the junction station. Two separate railways serving Havant and within such a short distance of Hayling Island might have led to a new connection to the island but continued wrangling rendered it unlikely that any transport would be offered. The failure gave local residents and tradesmen fresh impetus and meetings were held to engender support for the resurrection of a railway to Langstone and on to the island. Neither of the main line companies was interested in backing such a minor scheme, but with determined efforts a local company was formed. Despite objections by the Portsmouth and Arundel Navigation Committee, the LSWR and two landowners, the company was incorporated by the Hayling Railways Act on 23rd July, 1860 (23 and 24 Vict. cap. clxvi) being empowered to build two railways; the first a railway, wholly in the County of Southampton,

> … commencing by a junction with the main line of the LBSCR at a point situate 26 chains or thereabout eastward of Havant station of that railway in the Parish of Warblington and Havant, or one of them, and passing through the Parishes of Warblington, Havant, North and South Hayling, and Langston and terminating, at or near the Ferry House at Cumberland Ferry in the Parish of South Hayling in the Island of Hayling on Sinah Common.

The second railway, wholly in the County of Southampton commenced,

> … by a junction with the Direct Portsmouth Railway at a point 52 chains or thereabouts northward of the point of the junction of that railway with the LBSCR in the Parish of Havant, and passing through the Parishes of Havant and Warblington and terminating by junction with the intended railway first described, at a point at or near where the said intended railway is intended to pass under the Turnpike Road leading from Havant to Chichester, in the said parish of Havant.

The route was to follow the original planned line of 1851 to Langstone before crossing the intervening Langstone Harbour by a wooden trestle bridge, 960 ft in length, with a swivel opening bridge across the channel, which would allow two openings of not less than 40 ft span, with the soffit of the open pile work not less than 8 ft above the high water mark at spring tides to enable shipping to continue to use the local quay. Once across the bridge the railway was to continue on an embankment alongside the west shore of the island so as to reclaim over 1,000 acres of mudflats, which would become Crown Lands suitable for agricultural and residential use. It was thought that by providing its own embankment the company would save the expense of purchasing land on the island for the railway. Over the distance of 3 miles and 4 furlongs from the high water mark at Langstone to the terminus near the south end of Hayling, the railway and other works were not to deviate from the continuous centre line of way marked on the plans deposited with the Admiralty without the previous written consent of the Lord High Admiral of the United Kingdom of Great Britain and Ireland or the Commissioners for executing the Office of the Lord High Admiral. During the construction of the bridge the company was compelled by clause xxvi of the Act, to exhibit navigational lights for the guidance of vessels and thereafter on completion of the structure from sunset to sunrise. The following clause required the railway company not to detain unnecessarily any vessel navigating the channel for a longer period of time than to allow the passage of a train across the bridge, on penalty of £10 for any detention caused.

The Hayling Railway was not to take lands of the LSWR and LBSCR at Havant, neither were they to interfere with the operations at the junction without prior consent of the respective Engineers. All works at the junction were to be supervised by and installed to the satisfaction of the LBSCR or LSWR Engineers and if any obstruction or interference was proved the company was liable to a fine of £50 per hour. By Clause xlvii the LSWR was granted running powers over the Hayling Railway using its own locomotives and stock.

The Act authorized the raising of £50,000 in £10 shares, with borrowing powers of £16,600 once half the capital had been raised. Three years were allowed for purchasing the necessary land and four years for the completion of works. The Directors appointed by the Hayling Railway were Thomas Paris, Frederick Twynam, Louis More and Robert Watkins, whilst James Abernethy was appointed Engineer, Thomas J. Hay Resident Assistant and G.T. Porter, Solicitor. The contract for building the line was awarded to Frederick Furniss but no construction commenced until the spring of 1863 and by the autumn it was evident, by reason of a perilous infancy, that an extension of time would be required.

The initial meeting of the Hayling Railway Directors was held at 4 Victoria Street, Westminster, London SW on 1st July, 1863 with Frederick Twynam as Chairman, and fellow Directors Denton and Paris in attendance. Denton tendered his resignation and Compton Reade and Silas Taylor were appointed Directors. The common seal of the company was affixed to the agreement with the contractor Frederick Furniss to construct the line, whilst Robert Hicks was appointed as temporary company secretary. Two days later at a meeting at the company offices 61 Lincoln's Inn Fields, Twynam and Taylor both resigned and George Gowland, George Bragington and Sir Henry Leeke were appointed Directors, with Samuel Oldfield as Secretary and Glyn Mills and Company, bankers. On 8th July it was agreed that the company's Prospectus would be advertised in no less than 22 national and local newspapers, including *The Times, The Telegraph, The Standard, The Daily News, Hampshire Advertiser, Hampshire Independent, Hampshire Telegraph, Isle of Wight Express, Portsmouth Times, Portsmouth Chronicle, Sussex Express, Sussex Advertiser, West Sussex Gazette, Leeds Mercury, Birmingham Journal, Glasgow Herald, Morning Star, Manchester Examiner, Manchester Guardian, Liverpool Daily Post, Liverpool Mercury* and the specialist journals including *Herapath's Journal* and the *Railway Times.*

Conscious that the period allowed by the statute for the purchase of property had expired, urgent approaches were made in early August 1863 to acquire land and it was resolved that the solicitor should consult with Frederick Furniss before making any agreement or purchase. A month later on 2nd September the Secretary was authorized to issue paid up shares to the contractor in lieu of cash as payment of monthly certificates, if there was insufficient cash in the bank. At the same meeting the settlement of a claim by the Hayling Bridge Co. was agreed subject to the consent of Furniss.

Unfortunately the necessary capital was not forthcoming, and a new Board of Directors appointed comprising Admiral Sir Henry Leeke, who had originally opposed the railway, George Gowland, Compton Reade and George Bragington were forced to seek Parliamentary authority to extend the period for the purchase of land and completion of works and indeed make the company and the railway more attractive to developers. At this time Samuel Oldfield was Secretary, whilst James Abernethy was Consultant Engineer and Thomas Hay, Acting Engineer.

On a brighter note work on the authorized railway was progressing slowly but satisfactorily, supervised by engineers Hayter and Jay, despite exorbitant prices being demanded for the necessary land. Even when prices were agreed and the property acquired the contractor had to wait until crops had been harvested. It was also agreed to extend the railway for a distance of just over a mile beyond the terminus to a point on the coast where a pier and docks could be constructed. On 6th October, 1863 Thomas Hay was instructed to survey the extension and prepare the necessary plans for presentation to the Parliamentary private bill office. By 18th November the survey was completed and plans prepared and the requisite notice of the extension of the line and construction of pier and docks approved. The Directors agreed to lay the Bill before Parliament to authorize an extension of the share capital to £300,000 and the raising of debentures to £83,000, in addition to the £16,600 borrowing powers authorized in the 1860 Act. It was agreed that a new Prospectus would be prepared and steps taken to invite public subscription for the increased capital. At the meeting James Abernethy was appointed company Engineer. A week later on 25th November W.H. Wilson was appointed to replace Samuel Oldfield as company Secretary and the company's office was transferred to Wilson's address at 6 Victoria Street, London SW. Furniss submitted his fifth completion certificate in respect of excavations, piling and fencing to the value of £7,565 and it was noted that the four earlier certificates, for which payment had been made, totalled £7,219.

On 11th January, 1864 agreement was reached with Furniss for construction of the extension, but in the meantime he was urged to continue with the authorized railway. By March an approach was made to the Admiralty as the contractor wished to commence work on the swing bridge at Langstone. However, on 16th March it was pointed out that if the Admiralty consented to construction in the manner proposed by the company Engineer, an agreement would have to be prepared whereby the company would have to agree to alter the bridge construction in such a manner as the Admiralty may think necessary, if any obstruction was caused to the tidal flow or channel at Langston. At the same meeting it was revealed that the original estimates allowed for 63 lb. per yard rails but the contractor was authorized to substitute these with 80 lb. per yard rails.

Furniss wrote to the Board proposing a slight deviation from the original plans and the matter was considered on 26th May, 1864. The Board approved, as they considered the deviation would assist the future construction of the docks by enclosing the cove at Hayling Point and the resultant spoil from the docks would assist in the construction of the extension. The contractor's 10th certificate for £21,203 was presented for payment on 1st July, 1864 and included timber for the viaduct, incorporating 3,810 cu. ft under 'works' and 13,675 cu. ft 'materials on the ground', as well as wrought iron for the turnpike overbridge and the cost of deviation at No. 2 level crossing.

The Hayling Dock and Railway Act 1864 (27 and 28 Vict. cap. 177) received the Royal Assent on 14th July, 1864 and authorized a 1¼ mile extension of the railway from Sinah Point to Sea View Terrace, South Hayling, a development as yet unbuilt, and the provision of docks and a pier near the ferry terminal. Two years were allowed for completion of the railway and five years for the ambitious docks scheme. The statute authorized the raising of £10,000 for general purposes, £60,000 for the docks development and £6,000 for the railway extension, with borrowing powers equal to £25,300. Agreement could be sought with the LSWR or LBSCR for the working of the railway. This Act also authorized a 27 chains-long connection with the LBSCR, forming a junction with its main line at the east end of Havant station and crossing New Lane, Havant by a level crossing. The following month the engineers erroneously reported that the line could be opened for goods traffic to the small quay at Langstone, whilst the Directors were advised that the contractor was employing additional manpower and wagons on the southern part of the line.

At a meeting on 10th November, 1864 the solicitor was instructed to write to the LBSCR & LSWR Joint Committee seeking a possible working agreement. A fortnight later on 24th November the Directors considered a letter from Furniss regarding the Engineer's requirements for earthworks. These were to vary from two feet to six feet higher than originally specified and would involve him in serious loss. Furniss reiterated he was already working under difficulties in consequence of the share capital not having been subscribed as represented it would be. The Board considered the matter and requested the Engineer and Furniss to specify the exact quantity of the earthworks in the embankment when finally constructed. While they did not feel justified in paying for a larger quantity of soil than originally specified, they were prepared to pay for any additional timber casing to the bank. At the same meeting the Engineer reported progress of works. From Havant station the cutting had been taken out to formation level for the whole length, banks were formed and the permanent way laid throughout and also fastened to the viaduct over the Langstone estuary, a distance of 1½ miles. The cutting was not altogether completed, as the slopes were left upright to provide material for further earthworks and ballasting. Plans for the junction had been submitted to the LBSCR Engineer and his modification agreed to. When the final sanction was given it was expected that the LBSCR would install the necessary pointwork. Some complaints had been made regarding the length of the level crossing at Cemetery Lane, Havant. The viaduct had the floor laid up to the central channel and on the Hayling Island side of the structure the piles were driven and struts and longitudinals fixed on 13 of the 25 bays. It was expected that this work would be completed by Christmas. The Engineer then advised that part of the swivel bridge for the channel had arrived, and the remainder promised within three weeks. The contractor would expedite the fixing of the span as it was necessary for passing his earth wagons between the viaduct and the bank constructed from the side cutting on Hayling Island, where a length of 9½ chains had to be filled in. Arrangements had been made for a locomotive to proceed with this work and the 'completion of the viaduct and swing bridge was the sole hindrance to its immediate employment'. Outstanding work included a length of bank 2⅛ miles long, the construction of sluices for drainage, the fixing of the swing bridge, the construction of stations and associated works and the completion of the permanent way.

When questioned as to a possible date for opening, the Engineer recommended against opening to passenger traffic to Langston, as this could not be justified. He thought correctly that the Board of Trade (BoT) sanction might not be necessary for goods traffic only. Some coal would still have to be unloaded at the Old Quay, necessitating opening the bridge, but he recommended the construction of a siding to the quay for the Langstone Bridge Co. The levels in the Parliamentary plans had been miscalculated and failed to allow for the tidal rise and fall, hence necessitating the increase in the depth of the bank. The contractor was asked to construct the siding at Langstone to enable the transfer of coal to the railway. Terms were to be arranged with the Langstone Quay Co. as to receipt of such coals, free of haulage rates with not less than 500 tons of coal to be delivered to the siding on 2nd January, 1865.

Thomas Hay, now resident Engineer, reported to the Board meeting on 8th December, 1864 the additional costs incurred as a result of changes in specification: £1,340 for the substitution of 80 lb. per yard rails, £900 for Langstone Quay siding,

£1,720 for sundry deviations, gradient changes and the increased height of the bank, £200 for additional timber fenders to protect the swing bridge from vessels, £300 for the provision of a footbridge at Palmers Lane and £2,000 for a public road bridge at Langston in place of the level crossing if required by the Board of Trade. The Board would not commit themselves to payment of Furniss's extra claims but in view of the anticipated opening of the line to Langston for goods traffic on 10th January, 1865 and the need for additional siding and station accommodation, they made a further advance to Furniss by the issue of debentures. As the company proceeded with plans to open the line F.D. Banister, the LBSCR Engineer, complained that Hay's plan of the junction at Havant was incomplete with regard to curves and layout. At the Board meeting on 21st December Hay was directed to complete the plan without undue delay so as not to jeopardize the opening on 10th January, 1865. However, in the New Year small differences had yet to be resolved and on 5th January it was announced that opening would be put back to 12th January, 1865.

The first mile of the horse-drawn railway was opened for goods traffic only between Havant and Langstone on 12th January, 1865 and a considerable tonnage of timber, coal, gravel and general merchandise was conveyed from the quay at Langstone to various destinations. The opening of the single line section presented no problems to the Hayling company but receipts for the first five weeks of operation only averaged £10 per mile per week. During the ensuing months the constant tidal movements within Langstone Harbour eroded away complete sections of the unconsolidated embankment of the proposed line on the western shores of Hayling, leaving the company no alternative but to seek the abandonment of the scheme for the southern half of the line.

When Furniss submitted his 16th certificate on 9th February, 1865 his total expenditure on works amounted to £34,117. At the Board meeting on 7th April, 1865 Admiral Sir Percy Leake was re-elected Chairman of the Hayling Railway, with A.P. Barlow Deputy Chairman and Messrs Gowland and Reade forming the Executive Committee. On 13th April, Furniss made written application for a further advance payment in the form of shares and debentures to enable him to meet payments. 'I shall have a second engine on the line in a few days. My engineer left last Saturday to fetch her home and he writes me that he will be at Havant, he thinks about Thursday next'. The payment was approved, as was certificate No. 17 payment, which brought the total expenditure to £37,546.

Furniss presented his 18th certificate for payment on 31st May, 1865, bringing the total expended to £39,801. He also appealed for additional money to enable Langston swing bridge to be completed:

My outlay is very great now and I cannot possibly do anything with the ordinary shares to facilitate my carrying out the works. The issuing of preference shares would be some little advantage and as there is an item of some £9,000 for extras, which must be paid in preference shares it is most desirable this should be taken into consideration as early as possible as I shall have the bridge complete now in about three weeks, when I shall have a strong workforce on at the Havant end in addition to a large force I have on at the Hayling end, and an engine going at each point. I have also barges delivering material out to the site of the embankment in large quantities, all of which have to be paid for in cash. I am in a position to make a great push now and look forward with full hope of completing the bank by the end of September.

The solicitor also wrote that before midsummer he had to settle claims for £4,000 for land, otherwise several bills would be filed against the company. He explained that

Furniss had only paid about £1,300, and the total cost including land on the south side of the bridge was more than double his estimate of £3,000.

On 29th June, 1865 Messrs Hume and Stone were appointed new Directors. At the meeting Furniss was asked to supply a statement of the gross receipts earned since the opening of the railway, as the traffic returns already received were 'most unsatisfactory'. It was resolved that Messrs Gowland and Reade would attend Havant and ascertain what steps could be taken to improve the position of the company. A little over a week later on 5th July the Engineer reported 'further progress as slight' which did not warrant the issue of a further certificate. Little progress was made fixing the bridge and measures for stopping Sinah Lake were not vigorously prosecuted. He considered that the bridge would require three weeks' work to completion and about the same time for closing the lake. He estimated 22 weeks were required for completion of not less than 110,000 cubic yards of earth for the bank and the laying of the permanent way beyond Langston bridge. 'To do this will require considerable exertion on the contractor's part.' He finally suggested the Board approach the solicitor regarding the powers that could be enforced on Furniss to complete the line. The Board members were extremely dismayed at the lack of progress and resolved to call Furniss to account for the delay and to ascertain from the contractor when the line could be open for goods traffic to Sinah Lake. Consideration was also to be given to the steps required to construct a landing place or jetty for goods traffic at Sinah Lake.

By 13th September, 1865 the company's affairs were in a serious state. Correspondence was read regarding land purchases, the seizure by the Sheriff for land monies due to Messrs Clarke and Hitchens and the general financial requirements of the contractor. The Board, without prejudice to the contract or contractor's liability authorized the advance of £500 in cash and £2,000 in shares to Furniss, in advance of certificates on condition that the contractor at once enabled the solicitor to discharge the land claims for which execution was now issued. Furniss duly replied with reference to the authority to issue him with certain debentures for three years in exchange for others at seven years to the total of £10,300 and requested the amount be increased by £1,500 and this the Board agreed on 10th November.

Twelve days later the Board considered a letter from Thomas Hay requesting further alterations. The Board replied they could not sanction any alterations in the contract or openings (culverts) in the bank, without a proper agreement with Furniss and Mr Hume. However, they agreed they would accept responsibility for the extra maintenance costs of such openings or the filling in should this become necessary.

In the New Year work on the railway stuttered to a halt but it was 26th February, 1866 before the solicitor advised that four landowners had laid claim for outstanding payments against the company, totalling £2,822 and it was anticipated they would soon take action. Furniss had been asked whether he was prepared to recommence the works and carry out his contract but declined. After discussing the company's position with regard to the four judgements and the levy on the line made by the Sheriff of Hampshire, the Directors held Furniss fully responsible for all damage, which might arise from his non-fulfilment of contract. Unless he resumed work on the railway within 14 days the Board would take such steps to continue such works with a new contractor. In a letter dated 14th February, 1866, Hay reported he had visited the line the previous Monday and noted the works remained much the same as they were on 16th January when he had submitted his previous report and no appreciable work had been completed since that date. 'The recent severe gales, especially that of last Sunday, have done a little damage, but on the whole the works have stood up well to the strain.' The distance between the two 'tips' along the course laid out, which was somewhat longer in order to avoid soft places or springs, was about 2 miles 8 chains and he estimated the quantity requiring to be tipped was 120,000 cubic yards. The viaduct over Sinah Lake was solidly constructed but Hay was desirous of knowing whether this was acceptable in lieu of a closed bank. The Directors, whilst noting the report, requested full and complete details and plans, to show the amount of work done and the amount represented by each completion certificate and the time necessary for completion. At the general meeting which immediately followed the Board meeting, the Directors decided that Messrs Barlow and Reade and also Mr Crowley, who was elected to the Board that day, any two of them, with Mr Hume, could form a committee to negotiate and make such arrangements as were necessary to assist the company in its present financial difficulties.

Unfortunately the position further deteriorated. Furniss had moved back to Southsea to complete drainage works employing some 400 men, for his letter of 28th February, 1866 c/o Main Drain Works Contractor's Office, Wish House, Southsea (previous letters were from Hayling Railway Company Contractor's Office, Havant), pointing out that the works were never suspended, although, 'he might have well done so considering the great inconvenience and loss he had sustained owing to those connected with the undertaking not fulfilling their engagements'. He asked the Board to note that he had given up his establishment in Havant and future correspondence was to be directed to Southsea. The letter was noted at the HR Board meeting on 7th March, 1866 when Reade resigned his Directorship. As requested Hay submitted his report on progress although he pointed out that the company's request for his opinion of the position of the contractor in relation to the company was 'hardly a question for the Engineer, except as to the part of the line completed and that still to be done'. Hay's report showed the precarious state of the works.

At Havant, a junction has been made with the LBSCR and a siding put in. Earthworks thence to the viaduct over Langston Channel are completed to formation level. One mile 42½ chains of cutting require ballasting to finish it, also an engine turntable and further accommodation sidings required here, whilst the station platform at Havant needs lengthening. Regarding his report of 7th December, 1865 a timber fender was still required but was on order, but no further news had been received as to the need for two bridges mentioned. The viaduct and bridge are completed except for handrails and gravel boards. From the viaduct end the bank has been tipped to 1 mile 72½ chains, where there is gap of 2 chains, then the bank is completed to 2 miles 41 chains. There follows an opening of 2 miles 8 chains, which brings us the vexed question as to a timber viaduct or a solid earth bank over Sinah Lake, with the need or not for the construction of sluices and this is for the Directors to decide. So much of the timber viaduct - about 300 ft - so far built is of solid construction. From the end of this a bank 46 chains long has been tipped and permanent rails distributed, which brings us to the end of the line at Sinah. Over the bank, when completed, permanent way and ballasting is to be carried out also the facing of slopes and construction of the station at Sinah. The line cannot therefore be properly completed in less than seven months from now.

The Directors found the position unacceptable but a further shock awaited the company and especially Furniss when a series of advertisements appeared in the *Portsmouth Times*. The initial entry for 3rd March, 1866 read,

The Hayling Island Railway, Hayling and Havant. To contractors, iron merchants and others. On Friday next King and King are in receipt of instructions, under an execution from the Sheriff of Hampshire to sell by auction (unless the claim is previously settled) on the works on Friday 9th March, 1866 at 12.00, several tons of railway metal, several thousand sleepers, about 100 trolley wagons and general plant. Catalogues from Auctioneer or Sheriff's Offices.

Then on 10th March, 1866 a letter to the newspaper stated,

We shall be glad if you will allow us the opportunity of stating through your columns, that in the sale of plant advertised by us last week to have taken place at Hayling on Friday, and since postponed, the execution of the Sheriff of Hampshire was not levied against Mr Furniss the contractor, but against the Hayling Railway Company. We feel it due to Mr Furniss to give this explanation as unexplained the advertisement was probably calculated to do him an injury and an injustice. Yours, King and King.

Further correspondence on 17th March read,

To Railway Companies, Contractors, Iron Merchants and Others. The Hayling Railway Company, King and King are in receipt of instructions under certain writs of *fieri-facias* from the Sheriff of Hampshire, to sell by auction on the Iron Bridge at Langston, on Wednesday next 21st March, 1866 at 12 o'clock, unless the writs of execution be previously satisfied - a large quantity of iron rails and railway metals, of the kind known as bridge rails, forming or intended to form the permanent way of the railway. Catalogues from Auctioneers or Sheriff's Offices.

There is no further indication of the sale having taken place, so presumably the writs were satisfied.

Before the auction, the Directors had on 9th March, 1866, considered a further report from Hay. He advised that the total contract amounted to £59,179 and the amount certified by completion certificates totalled £39,454, leaving a balance of £19,725. The full estimate of the completion of the railway, including 'stations, simple in character, containing booking office, waiting room, lamp room, closets' was £2,001, platforms £850 and he estimated completion of the line could be achieved with expenditure of £13,500.

The turbulent affairs of the railway abated, but away from the public gaze much was astir. On 30th July, 1866 the Secretary reported on the affair of Mr Daniell's claim in Chancery for settlement of land purchase where the court had ordered the company to make a declaration in answer to certain questions to avoid further proceedings. After referring to the certificates he could not endorse the declaration made by the company's solicitor and stressed that amendments were necessary to settle the matter. Letters were also received from James Abernethy's solicitor regarding outstanding payment of a claim for consulting engineering services and most importantly a letter from a Francis Fuller offering to purchase the line.

Francis Fuller, a London land and estate agent, had visited Hayling Island in connection with the clearing of estate problems on the death of Mr Padwick. He at once realised the potentiality of the natural beauty and charm of the area with the possibility of furthering its standing as a holiday resort. Purchasing some land near the south beach he also promoted a racecourse as an attraction for summer visitors. Only transport remained a problem, and here was a railway with works suspended, exposed to wind, weather and waves and almost bankrupt. The Hayling Railway

Directors were at a loss to decide their next move when the astute Fuller arrived on the scene to infuse new lifeblood into the ailing company. After long and patient negotiations with the Board he rallied the ranks of shareholders to action. The folly of running a railway on an embankment offshore was pointed out and Fuller agreed to purchase the necessary land close to the west shore of the island for the line, thus clearing the main obstacle against completion.

At the Board meeting on 31st October, 1866 chaired by Barlow, and with Hume and Crowley, fellow Directors, Francis Fuller was duly elected a Director of the company. Barlow offered his resignation but was pressed to remain on the Board by Fuller. A letter submitted by the solicitor informed the gathering that a notice of injunction restraining the company from using the railway had been tendered and the embargo was to remain in force unless the purchase money in the case brought by Daniell against the Hayling Railway was paid up. The solicitor pointed out he had defended this and other proceedings as long as possible and met counsel's fees himself but was now requesting reimbursement. It was resolved that Daniell's suit be settled, also Woodcock's claim for £50 for land purchase. The solicitor was instructed to obtain from Mr Furniss a return of all traffic receipts since the opening of the line, the balance of which less working expenses was to be paid to the company's bankers.

Fuller, having purchased land on Hayling, suggested a deviation from the authorized route obviating the tremendous earthworks required on the west coast of the island south of the bridge and agreed to meet Furniss and arrange with him the construction of the deviation. No arrangement was to be authorized unless it included complete settlement of any claim by Furniss against the Hayling Co. in respect of works already executed or disputed by the Board, the company having been advised of entitlement to damages from the contractor for non-compliance of his contract dated 1st July, 1863. After prolonged negotiations it was agreed that notice was to be forwarded to Parliament for a Bill:

1. To authorize a proposed deviation from Langston bridge.
2. Application of the capital authorized in the Act of 1864 for the purposes of such deviation and to raise further monies.
3. Renewal of the powers of the Acts of 1860 and 1864 for the construction works and docks and extension of time.
4. To enable arrangements with any other Railway Company promoting an extension of the Hayling Railway to Southsea or other places.

Barlow's resignation was finally accepted on 20th November, 1866 and Francis Fuller became Chairman. He reported on his meeting with Furniss, who required more cash payments than the Board was prepared to offer. It was agreed the works of the railway were to be priced and a fresh report made. A meeting of bondholders was tentatively arranged for 4th December, to advise on the steps to be taken for the completion of the railway but in the meantime the new Chairman recommended the appointment of Mr Whittaker as architect for the Sinah bridge scheme. He would be reimbursed with two-third preference shares and one-third ordinary shares for his services.

The bondholders meeting was subsequently cancelled and arrangements made for Mr Campbell to act as their representative. It was announced at the Board meeting on 5th December, 1866 that Furniss was willing to complete the works according to the new plans for £10,000 receiving as payment one-third cash, one-third preference shares and one-third ordinary shares, on condition that the timber used on Sinah viaduct and stock and materials included in the engineer's certificate be considered his property. The solicitor was instructed to prepare a Bill for extension No. 1 from Langston to the south end of the iron bridge towards the sea beach at the point agreed on the estate of Captain Haunton at Hayling. At the end of the year the solicitor pointed out that the claims of Daniell and others amounting to £444 plus £59 costs were still not settled and they were empowered to stop traffic on the line. Steps were to be taken to settle the claims. The solicitor also raised the subject of the declaration of funds and pointed out that with regard to the new Bill for the 1867 session, the costs of such undertaking being a substituted line of railway were to be defrayed from the £66,000 authorized by the Hayling Railway Act of 1860, and the Hayling Railways and Docks Act 1864, and the £21,000 borrowing powers, of which upwards of £34,000 remained unexpended.

Francis Fuller had also advised the LBSCR of his interests in the Hayling Railway and sought that company's opinion on a possible working agreement. The matter was raised at the LBSCR Directors meeting on 11th December, 1866 when the Secretary was directed to reply that the company was prepared to enter in to arrangements to work the line at prime cost, subject to certain rebate arrangements.

Then on 12th February, 1867 Hawkins, the LBSCR Secretary, submitted to the LBSCR Board a letter received from the LSWR asking for a meeting regarding the Hayling Railway. Hawkins was directed to meet Scott of the LSWR to talk the matter over but not to agree to anything. The Secretary was also instructed to report at the next Board meeting on whether the Hayling Railway was a prohibited district in respect of joint working between the LSWR and LBSCR. A week later on 19th February the Secretary submitted a map attached to the agreement made with the LSWR in 1859 which pointed out that the Hayling Railway was in the LBSCR's district, but that there was a clause in the agreement which stated that: 'notwithstanding such distribution and appropriation if any line of railway be hereafter made from Havant or thereabouts to Langston Harbour, the LSWR shall be at liberty to make arrangements for running over, and using such line for traffic of all kinds from this railway to and from Langston Harbour'.

In the meantime the Hayling Railway Directors were optimistic of progress. After much negotiation it was announced on 25th February, 1867 that Furniss, on the understanding that all claims on either side were abandoned, was willing to complete the construction of the railway from Langston to Hayling at a cost of £3,875, and then to maintain the permanent way and works in good order for a period of 12 months after opening for £120. The solicitor also announced that on the total payment of £45, £5 to the Commoners of Creek Common and £40 to Mr Crasweller, owner and occupier, the company could have immediate possession of the land required for the railway on the west coast of the island opposite Langston and South Hayling, so that the contractor could at once fence off the line of formation and proceed with the work. The Commoners of Creek Common then advised that they would grant freehold of their portion of land for a one-off payment of £250 and to this the company readily agreed. The only cloud on the horizon was the opposition to the new Bill raised by the LSWR, an oyster company and Mr Gale. It was reluctantly agreed to defer the construction of the deviation until the opposing parties had withdrawn their opposition. The railway company subsequently entered into an agreement with the oyster company on 22nd March, 1867 whereby the Hayling Railway Bill should not be read for the third time in the House of Lords until a lease was agreed between the interested parties involved with mudflats on the west side of the island and embankments used for oyster cultivation. John Bullar was delegated to negotiate with the interested parties regarding the lease of the mudflats, the railway bank on the west side of the oyster beds and a bank on the north side formerly used as a contractor's road. The railway company was to take up the existing rails and substitute 50 lb. per yard rail and sleepers, which would then become the property of the oyster company. Whilst expanding in area the oyster company also sought powers to bridge the railway. All was nullified as far as the railway was concerned for Bullar died before completing the lease agreement. The original route was to be abandoned in favour of a route passing to the east of the mudflats and later skirmishes did not involve the company save that they had to maintain and keep in good repair the railway embankment.

On 4th March, 1867 the Hayling Railway Secretary sent a letter to the Joint Committee of the LBSCR and LSWR suggesting the leasing of the Hayling Railway to either or both companies. In furtherance of the offer it was pointed out that a land company, with a capital of £200,000, was about to purchase the whole of the sea frontage at Hayling and a large quantity of land behind it with a view to forming a considerable watering place. 'As Hayling had the advantage of being an excellent bathing place with shady walks and drives, it may be assumed that the place will grow rapidly and become of considerable advantage to the interests of both companies'. It added, 'Powers were being sought for altering the course of the Hayling Railway from Langston to Hayling and as landowners were not only assenting but anxious to have the line made, they had consented to allow their line to be used at once, and it can therefore be constructed', optimistically forecasting 'opening by 1st June next, so that a considerable amount of traffic may be obtained in the summer and autumn if Hayling can be brought within two hours of London by arrangement with your companies'. The letter assured,

... that 1,000 tons of coal per week would be taken from Langston inland by your lines of railway'. The cost of the railway is so far upwards of £60,000 and about £20,000 more is required to complete. In order to enable the directors to raise this £20,000 it is proposed that one or both of your companies should upon completion of the line to Board of Trade satisfaction take a lease of the property at £1,500 for first year, £2,000 for the next five years and £3,000 a year thereafter or if preferred should work the traffic for 50 per cent of the gross receipts and should give the Hayling Railway a rebate of 20 per cent on all traffic brought on their lines. Should either proposition be accepted there will be no difficulty raising the necessary capital and entering on the works.

It was also announced Furniss was willing to complete the line to Board of Trade satisfaction within three months from the date of receiving the order to proceed.

Frederick Furniss was indeed again employed as contractor for the southern half of the line and work on this relatively easy section commenced in the spring of 1867. The contractor's task over the flat terrain of the island was considered relatively easy and early completion of the railway ready for Board of Trade inspection was expected. Fuller meanwhile had purchased further land for property development near the South Beach and it was agreed on 7th May, 1867 that the company would repay Fuller's expenditure on the purchase of land, within three months of Parliament passing the new Bill. It was also agreed for part of the mud land at Hayling Island, over which the new line would run would be leased to the oyster company. Despite signs of progress, advancement of the railway was only made at a cost for in the same month John Gould of Gravesend was appointed Manager and Receiver of the Hayling line with a remit to stabilize the ailing finances.

On 14th June, 1867 the LBSCR deferred any further meetings between Hawkins and the LSWR Traffic Manager until there were further developments on the

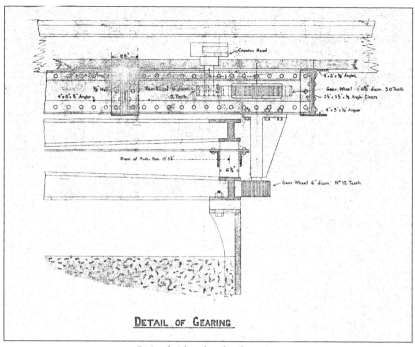

DETAIL OF GEARING

Swing bridge details of gearing

Swing bridge cross section

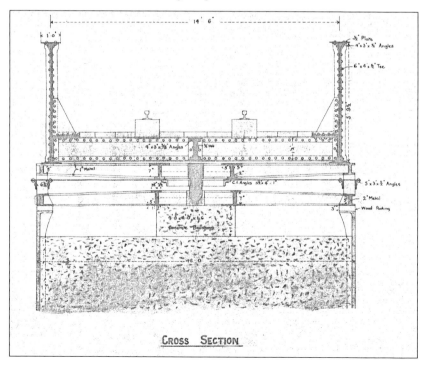

CROSS SECTION

Hayling Railway. Ten days later on 24th June the LBSCR Board considered a letter submitted by Sir Charles Fox and Messrs Few & Company on behalf of the Hayling Railway asking the sanction of the LBSCR to the formation of the physical junction between the two companies at Havant.

By 26th June, 1867 the Bill had passed the House of Commons Committee, a clause being inserted to secure the withdrawal of the opposition. Earlier in the month Sir Charles Fox had written two letters to Colonel Bartlett of the LBSCR requesting an alteration to the junction at Havant, so that trains from Hayling did not run on the LBSCR main line, as would undoubtedly be required by the Board of Trade. In the absence of a reply it was agreed that Sir Charles Fox would see Mr Laing, the new Chairman of the LBSCR, to obtain terms for effecting a junction and to open negotiations for working the line for three months from completion. Notice was also given to the Board of Trade signifying an expected opening of the line on 1st July, 1867. Such were the signs of progress that on 28th June, 1867 the first passenger train conveying VIPs including the Mayor of Portsmouth traversed the line and after arrival at the terminus guests enjoyed a meal at the Royal Hotel before returning to Havant.

Despite the passage of the special train the expected completion date for works was not achieved and at the LBSCR Board meeting on 2nd July the Traffic Manager reported on the junction the Hayling Railway wished to make at Havant. It appeared that permission was only sought to lay a siding, which would not prejudice the LBSCR rights in any way. As such he had consented to the installation of the siding to enable the Board of Trade inspector to inspect the line on 3rd July as proposed. It was resolved that the junction arrangements be approved and that Secretary Hawkins was to report fully on the larger question regarding the working of the railway by the LBSCR or LSWR inclusive of the use by the Hayling Railway of the LBSCR Havant station.

Colonel William Yolland duly carried out the Board of Trade inspection on 3rd July, 1867, noting that the line commenced at the Havant station of the LBSC, without making a junction with the main line and terminated at South Hayling station, a distance of 4 miles 37.61 chains. The line was single throughout with sidings at Havant and South Hayling and another at Langstone. The only overbridge and viaduct were constructed for single line but elsewhere the land was wide enough for double track. The width of the formation varied between 16 and 18 ft and the width between the lines where there were sidings was 6 ft. The one overbridge on the line was constructed of brick and the timber viaduct had an opening bridge constructed of iron with a 50 ft span. A the time of his visit Yolland did not have the Act of Parliament to refer to but was told the bridge did not comply with the statute, the sanction of the Board of Trade having been obtained to make an alteration. He commented, 'I have no reason to doubt the sufficiency of the strength of this iron bridge' but as no drawings were supplied he was unable to calculate the deflections in the structure. He noted the company was to supply additional drawings of the span as a matter of urgency. The inspector found no turntables had been installed at either Havant or South Hayling but as he understood it was to be worked as a local line, and not as a through line and the length was less than five miles, he considered that the Board of Trade would allow the dispensation of the turntables.

Yolland commented the line had been constructed and brought forward for inspection under 'somewhat peculiar circumstances', as only one portion 1 mile 55 chains in length from Havant to Langston was authorized for operation, but he noted there was a Bill before Parliament to legalize the remaining 2 miles 63.34 chains as a deviation from the original scheme. He understood the railway or a portion of it was already in the hands of a Receiver and Mr Scott, the General

LBSCR drawing of Langston swing bridge opening section.

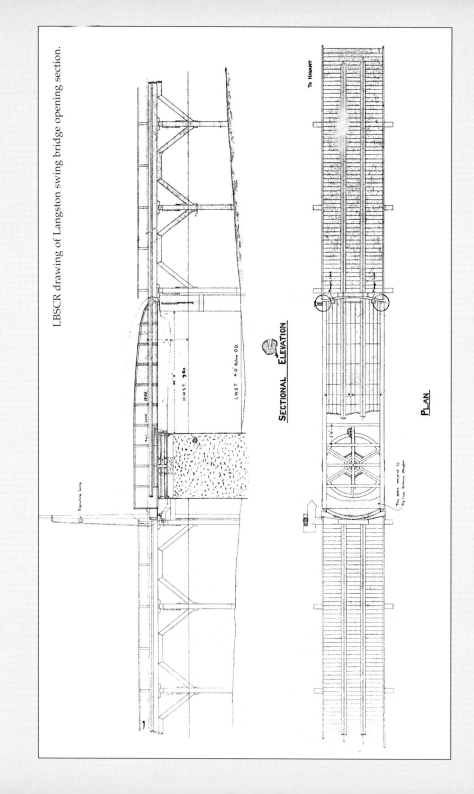

SECTIONAL ELEVATION

PLAN

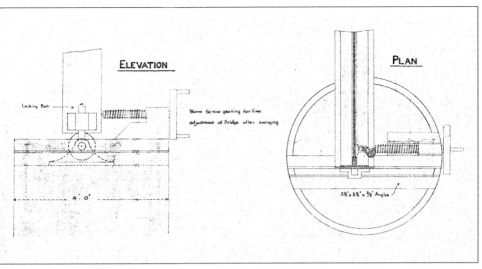

Swing bridge details of locking control and adjustment gearing

Swing bridge details of plunger lock.

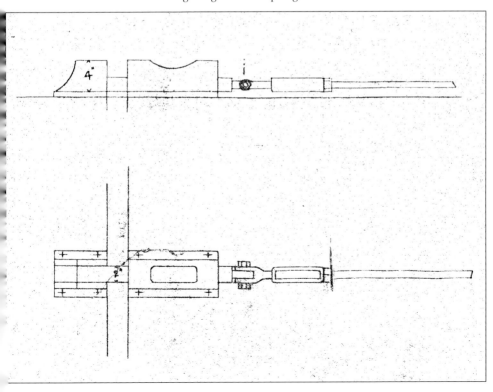

Manager of the LSWR had informed that his company and the LBSCR had running powers over the new line as the Hayling Railway did not possess any rolling stock nor had arrangements been made regarding the working of the line. The Colonel also had not received any undertaking as the mode of working the single track railway. At the conclusion of the inspection Yolland specified the following requirements to bring the line up to standard:

1. The sanctioned portion of the railway has been made up for some considerable time and it requires to be overhauled, thoroughly lifted and packed and the loop siding at Havant required for the engine to run round its train requires an indicator at its east end. The very sharp curve of 8 ½ chains radius must have a check rail provided throughout its whole length and the permanent way is very badly laid; the distant signal on the branch requires to be raised so that it may be better seen from the signalbox.

2. There is an unauthorised level crossing at 1 mile 8 ½ chains. The turnpike road was proposed to be crossed on the level when plans were deposited in 1859 but the then engineer of the line agreed to substitute a bridge when I saw him on the subject, and the level crossing was struck out of the bill.

3. The fencing is incomplete at many places along the line and the intermediate or brick posts are too far apart. There are some damaged rails and bad sleepers to be taken out and some bolts in the fishplates inserted here and there. The check rails opposite the crossing are not properly fitted and the facing points are not rightly adjusted.

4. A station signal is required to be placed at the points leading into Langston siding on which the distant signal from the opening bridge may work as a co-acting arm. These signals must lock the points open to the main line when they are off and thus Langston siding can only be entered or left when the signals are at danger.

5. The wooden viaduct requires to be carefully overlooked and some bolts are wanted where they are spiked, other bolts screwed up and the seating of the washing pieces properly secured. The opening bridge must be better secured and supported when a train is to traverse it and some additional piles are required to shelter the iron cylinders from vessels. The embankment adjacent to the wooden viaduct requires widening and protecting from the wash of the sea.

6. The southern portion of the line has been begun and finished in a very short space of time and it requires to be well looked over and lifted and packed in places, after some heavy engines have run upon it. It is very rough at present and the portion where the shingle is used as ballast must have gravel in addition. In other parts there is a deficiency of ballast.

7. The points leading only into the goods yard at South Hayling have been laid in and I presume it is intended that this yard should be completed, a signal will be required worked from the platform to control the departure of a train from the yard.

He concluded, 'I think it is of great importance from the peculiar circumstances which I have mentioned that the line should be put into thoroughly good order before it is opened to traffic and I have therefore only to report that by reason of incompleteness of the works, the opening of the Hayling Railway for traffic would be attended with danger to the public using the same'.

Meanwhile on 5th July, 1867, Hawkins, the LBSCR Secretary, reported having met with the LSWR Traffic Manager regarding the Hayling Railway and it was agreed that the matter be placed before the Joint Committee.

The only substantial newspaper reference appeared in the *Hampshire Post* on 6th July, 1867:

Vigorous efforts are now being made to develop Hayling Island, difficulty of access has at last been surmounted on completion of the Hayling Island Railway, which was commenced some three years ago. An Act of Parliament was obtained as long ago as 1860 and works commenced, but various difficulties arose and at one time it was feared the undertaking would have to be abandoned. Thanks to the public spirit of Francis Fuller, a large owner of property in the island, the work was resumed by F. Furniss, Contractor, who has executed it promptly and energetically. The line commences by junction with the London Brighton and South Coast and London and South Western Railways at Havant, and crosses a channel from Langston to Hayling Island by means of a viaduct 400 yards long, and the ponds of the South of England Oyster Company, and follows the line of coast to Hayling, where it ends at present, but it is intended to continue to Sinah, opposite Cumberland Fort, so that when the project for connecting the opposite shores of Langston Harbour by means of a floating bridge are carried out, there will be communication between Chichester and Southsea via Hayling Island. The station at South Hayling is within five minutes of the Royal Hotel. It is in the Gothic style of architecture and is a pretty little structure. It is built of red and white brick and includes a booking office, a ladies room, a retiring room and Station Master's house, a signal house now being in the course of erection. The Contractor, notwithstanding many difficulties, has accomplished a nearly six months task in a third of the time and works were sufficiently advanced to admit of a train with the Contractor, Mr Fuller and a party of friends traversing the line for the first time on Coronation Day (Friday 28th June). The Company subsequently partook of the hospitality of the Contractor at the Royal Hotel. Mr Furniss presided, Mr C.J. Longcroft, Vice Chairman, with the Mayor of Portsmouth and F. Fuller were among those present.

At the meeting on 8th July, 1867 it was revealed that opposition by Mr Gale had prevented the third reading of the Bill, but it was hoped terms could be arranged. The cost of the extension of the line and works, including the installation of the telegraph as certified by Sir Charles Fox, was to be ascertained. Colonel Yolland had taken the only course possible by deferring the opening of the line but a memorial from the local residents and Havant Local Board of Health stated they wished the existing level crossing at Langstone to be retained as Hayling traffic was light and the road deviation and bridge was not necessary. The document was passed to the Board of Trade. Fuller wrote that at the first meeting of the new LBSCR Directors on 2nd July, 1867, the Chairman had ordered the works at Havant station to be carried out at once and men were subsequently dispatched from London Bridge for that purpose, on the understanding the Hayling Railway met the full costs. Sir Charles Fox thought the cost of the works would be considerably more than expected and he was endeavouring to get one of the parent companies to relieve him of such payments. Mr Scott of the LSWR presented a solicitor's letter of the previous May regarding the appointment of John Gould of Gravesend as Manager and Receiver of the Hayling Railway and he thought no leasing could take place without his consent. The letter was immediately referred to the solicitor.

On 10th July, 1867 the LBSCR Deputy Chairman reported that he had inspected the documents showing that the LSWR under the 1860 Hayling Railway Act had acquired running and working powers for that line and it was therefore too late to raise the question with the LSWR, which under its agreement with the LBSCR was apparently excluded from Hayling Island. As regards the question of working the railway jointly or otherwise it appeared unprofitable to work the line at present but that it might become a paying line at some distant period. He therefore recommended that on the question coming before the LBSCR/LSWR Joint

Committee at their next meeting they should agree to leave the promoters of the Hayling Railway to work the line themselves. In the event of the LSWR being determined to work it the LBSCR should allow them to do so alone without prejudice to the LBSCR's rights at a future date.

Fuller wrote to the Hayling Railway Board on 12th July stating that the bad work of Furniss on the new line and the subject of Colonel Yolland's complaints had been made good and the bridge strengthened to the Board of Trade requirements. The railway was ready for a further inspection on Monday next, except for the works at Havant station, which were being carried out by the LBSCR. A telegraph was quickly dispatched to LBSCR officials with a confirmative covering letter and Allen Sarle the LBSCR Secretary replied that the LBSCR would only carry out the work on receipt of £540 costs. Francis Fuller undertook to pay the amount within three months of completion in the event of the Hayling Railway failing to do so and the work continued.

Yolland having refused to allow the opening of the line returned on 15th July, 1867 and found that a considerable amount of work had been done in the fortnight since his previous visit. He commented that some lengths of fencing were incomplete and that the intermediate or brick posts for some considerable length had still to be provided. A number of broken rails also required replacing. The work of mixing gravel or ballast with the shingle at the south end of the line was incomplete. The packing of rails at the abutments of the swing bridge required careful looking after. 'The Engineer Mr Fox assured me these things would be attended to', and informed him the line was to be worked by the LSWR but 'nothing has been definitely settled as to the terms'. The inspector was far from happy with the state of the line but concluded, 'If their Lordships shall determine to allow the line to open, notwithstanding the unauthorised road crossing, I would recommend that the traffic should be worked at a moderate speed, not exceeding 20 mph until the line becomes consolidated, as the southern portion has been made in a short time and in a very hurried manner'.

The line was officially opened on 17th July, 1867, which fortunately coincided with the second day of the inaugural race meeting on Sinah Common. The *Hampshire Telegraph* of 17th July reported that on the first day of the two day event heavy rain fell and the 'discomfiture [sic] was considerably increased by the fact that there was no railway communication from Havant as had been anticipated, the government inspector it is said not having gone over the line the previous day according to the arrangements'. It added: the service from Havant to Hayling will be opened this morning'. The *Portsmouth Times* for Saturday 20th July, 1867 stated:

> Hayling Island Races Tuesday and Wednesday last, 16th and 17th. Although the race card was embellished with a conspicuous notice that frequent trains would run from Havant to Hayling, the Government inspector not having awarded his certificate, the branch although completed was not open for public traffic until the second day – a hitch causing temporary inconvenience to visitors. Plenty of conveyances were available at Havant.

Although references were made to the station at South Hayling timetables of the period showed the station as Hayling Island.

The Board of Trade letter of 19th July, 1867 confirmed the authority to open the line on the understanding that Colonel Yolland's requirements were attended to and that at some future date an Act of Parliament legalized the unauthorized level crossing at Langston. The report was discussed at the Hayling Railway Board meeting on 22nd July when it was also noted that Yolland had requested fencing repairs, additional ballasting at the south end of the line and packing of rails at the abutments of the swing bridge. Colonel Yolland had been informed that the line was to be worked by the LSWR but no terms were definitely settled and after urgent negotiations Frederick Furniss operated the services. As the southern portion of the line had been made in a short time and a hurried manner the Colonel had recommended a 20 mph speed limit and this was to be adhered to.

A notice was published in the same newspaper on 27th July, 1867: 'Hayling Island Railway: The line is now open for Traffic and Trains run at intervals throughout the day to Havant, in connection with the LBSCR and Portsmouth Direct Railway. SPECIAL TRAINS will be provided on very reasonable terms for pleasure parties. For arrangements apply to F. Furniss, Langston, Havant'.

An insight into the early operation of the line can be gleaned from an article published in the *Railway News* of 3rd August, 1867 as part of a series of a Railway Rambler, when the writer urged his readers to take 'a dog-day flight to a *terra incognita* called the Isle of Hayling'. The author and his companion travelled by the 8.20 am train from the LBSCR City terminus, presumably London Bridge, before changing at Horsham and connecting with the train to Portsmouth. 'After little more than an hour the train reaches Havant where there is a sign, Havant for Hayling, pointing to a siding. There, true enough, stands the Hayling train, as queer and quaint looking a train as ever we saw in our life.' The pair joined the train drawn by a 'donkey engine' belonging to 'Mr Furness, the contractor, who at present works the line.' The reader learned that the two terminal stations had only one station master 'who travels up and down on the train, working like a shuttle'. The station master also had a role as booking clerk, guard, porter, treasurer and ticket taker. The writer observed, 'however it appears in these early days the new service is not at all heavy.'

On the Hayling section of the journey it was noted the train kept close to the western shore on land 'that seems to have been reclaimed from the sea'. Large oyster beds could be seen in the distance as well as the beautiful countryside 'rather thickly wooded with numbers of pretty farms, houses and smaller homesteads peeping out from amidst the orchards and flower gardens'. Hayling station consisted of a 'chalet like cottage in the midst of a field and is reached in less than ten minutes, and it seems a strange place to be let out'. The two gentlemen were directed to the Royal Hotel and then enjoyed a walk 'through thickly shaded lanes to enjoy the wonderful views of the Isle of Wight, with the whole of the British Fleet lying on the calm waters between us and the opposite shore'.

The pair then set out to explore and considered the beach firm and free from shingle and therefore 'superior to Brighton' but were annoyed to see 'some half dozen ghastly homes near the beach'. East of the Royal Hotel were 'charming abodes with large gardens sheltering among the trees, including 'one immense mansion quite palatial in style but in harmony with the other properties'. G.G. Sandeman the London wine merchant, owned the house and whose company paid duty annually to the British Government for nearly 200,000 gallons of wine they imported. On returning to Hayling station the travellers were met by 'a melancholy looking navvy, temporarily in charge who seemed surprised to see customers'. He received the solemn address 'Fear not O porter of the future, there will come a time when crowds will be flocking down from the metropolis to this beautiful island'. Then the 'fierce snorting of the donkey engine' was heard as the train arrived at the station whence from a third class carriage on to the platform stepped one solitary person 'an ancient dame carrying a sack of potatoes'.

Somewhat belatedly, Parliamentary powers were granted on 12th August, 1867 (30 and 31 Vict. cap. 189) for the 2 miles 64 chains overland route, commencing 60 chains south of Langston viaduct and the abandonment of the docks and harbour scheme. The railway in its completed state as built by Furniss remained without major modifications until closure. Ironically the Act allowed one year for the purchase of land and authorized the raising of an additional £6,000 by shares.

On the same day, 12th August, the oyster company requested the raising of the embankment at North Hayling by 12 inches using surplus soil removed from the cutting at Havant. It was agreed the oyster company could have the soil without cost provided they were responsible for carrying out the work.

In October 1867 the Inland Revenue Commissioners requested payment of the passenger duty earned since the opening of the railway. A reply pointed out that the Hayling Railway was 'in the hands of a receiver and as such the company had received no income', the overall total of £87,185 expended on works £54,564 was offset by the original paid-up capital and a further £21,300 by capital raised for the 1864 project, leaving a deficit of £11,321.

On 27th November, 1867 Mr Rose (one of the Directors) reported on the state of the accounts between the LBSCR and Francis Fuller for work done at Havant for the Hayling Railway. Fuller's cheque for £3,242 was accepted in full settlement of the outstanding debt and Hawkins reported through the LBSCR Traffic Committee on rental terms and toll he would recommend for the Hayling Railway's future use of Havant station.

On 4th February, 1868 it was revealed that a letter submitted to the Board of Trade reiterated that the line as far as Langston Harbour had for some months past been in the hands of the Receiver. It further revealed that the contractor, who had been making for a private party a railway from Langston Harbour to Hayling, had organized a train service on both portions of line without the sanction of the Receiver, and incorrectly reported that 'the receiver had now I understand interfered to stop the running of the trains'. The train service was suspended for a few weeks after flooding undermined the permanent way at North Hayling but resumed when repairs were completed.

By June 1868 the Inland Revenue was still asking for passenger duty and on 24th of the month a reply was drafted to the effect the company had not received any working returns and the Secretary advised that the Receiver appointed by the Court of Chancery was the proper person to whom application should be made. On the same date it was revealed that Francis Furniss had assigned his interest in the extension railway to a Mr Crampton. The service continued to operate and at a shareholders' meeting held on 6th August, 1868 a resolution was passed to the Board of Trade seeking exemption for providing financial returns. This was refused on the grounds that the company had completed and opened its line throughout.

Train services from the opening day were worked by agreement, with Furniss providing the locomotives and using ancient LSWR rolling stock. Because of severe weather again washing away the ballast near North Hayling, and other track damage, the railway was closed to traffic in December 1868, only to be restored in August 1869 with a service of four trains in each direction when the terminal station was re-titled South Hayling. Furniss continued to work the line with ancient locomotives and coaching stock until 31st December, 1871.

By February 1869 the accounts of the company were prepared in accordance with the Regulation of Railways Act 1868 but the following footnote was added over the signature of F. Fuller, 'This amount does not include what may be due by the company for the extension of the railway from Langston to near the beach at Hayling'.

On 19th January, 1870 Francis Fuller, as the major shareholder, who had expended more than £12,000 of his own money, offered to sell the Hayling Railway to the LBSCR but the offer was declined. Then in November of the same year he again wrote suggesting he could secure the line for purchase by the LBSCR for £27,500. The LBSCR Board were not in favour and the matter was referred to the LSWR and LBSCR Joint Committee. In the meantime Fuller found a willing buyer for his shares and at the LBSCR Board meeting on 22nd November, 1871 a letter received from Louis Hoersheim submitted on behalf of himself and his friends advised that they had acquired nearly the whole of the interest in the Hayling Railway and were now practically sole owners of the company. It was the intention to clear all liabilities and offer the LBSCR a working arrangement whereby it could permanently secure the Hayling Railway as part of the LBSCR system. Following an interview with Hoersheim the LBSCR Board accepted the offer subject to certain conditions:

1. That the agreement be in a form acceptable to the LBSCR Company's solicitor.
2. Payment by the LBSCR shall consist of only £2,000 per annum in addition to the cost of maintenance and working of the Hayling Railway and that the company was not entitled to any part of surplus receipts.
3. As regards the surplus lands, the Hayling Company are to retain or dispose of only so much (if any) of such lands as in the opinion of the LBSCR Company shall not be required for the purposes of the Hayling Railway, including present and future stations and sidings and wharf accommodation and all other necessary requirements for the efficient working of the railway and also for doubling thereof by and at the cost of the LBSCR should they so desire.
4. The Hayling Company are not to do or assent to any act which shall in any way affect the right of the LBSCR to the sole use and benefit of the Hayling Railway and working thereof, and the LBSCR is to have the option of requiring that such a proportion of share capital and voting powers of the Hayling Railway shall be placed in the hands of nominees of the LBSCR Company for nominal consideration, and shall in the opinion of their solicitor be sufficient for the protection of the company's rights and interests.

On 5th December, 1871 John Brewer chaired the first meeting of the Hayling Railway for over two years. Philip Rose, however, was subsequently appointed Chairman and at a later extraordinary meeting the new share capital was authorized; £16,000 being wholly subscribed and owned by Louis F. Hoersheim, together with a loan of £5,300. The following day Hoersheim accepted the LBSCR's offer subject to a slight amendment to clause 4. Somewhat belatedly on 22nd December, 1871 M.A. Sharp was disqualified from his directorship having transferred his shares to Hoersheim. On New Year's Day the Hayling Railway ceased to be an operating company and all but finite control was handed to the LBSCR management, thus hopefully ensuring a brighter future for the short branch.

South Hayling station *circa* 1880, showing LBSCR 2-4-0T No. 359 *Hayling Island* with pre-Stroudley carriage stock. Notice the absence of a canopy over the platform, the bricks and gate in the goods yard and in the right background the engine shed and primitive signal.

National Railway Museum

Chapter Two

LBSCR Operation

In accordance with an agreement between the two companies dated 25th December, 1871, the Hayling Railway was leased to the London Brighton and South Coast Railway from 1st January, 1872 at a guaranteed rental to the smaller company of £2,000 plus £150 per annum. On 5th January, 1872 Philip Rose, later Sir Philip Rose, was appointed a Director in place of M.A. Sharp and on 30th January the seal of the Hayling Railway was affixed to the working agreement with the LBSCR. On 12th January copies of the agreement between the Hayling Railway and the LBSCR were sent to the LSWR and the seal was affixed on 24th January. On the same day it was agreed Mr Cardew would represent LBSCR interests on the Hayling Railway Board and it was also agreed that if they so desired Mr Sarle was at liberty to accept the post of Secretary of the Hayling company.

The LSWR Directors, however, were not satisfied with the working agreement and on 7th February, 1872 the LBSCR Directors agreed to receive a deputation. The LSWR Chairman and Directors duly attended on 21st February and expressed their dissatisfaction with the way the LBSCR had entered into the working agreement without the knowledge of the LSWR. After a lengthy discussion, the LBSCR Chairman explained the reasons which led to his company taking prompt action, being the absence of any assurance from the LSWR in response to the letter from the Brighton Company on 11th November, 1870, advising they would not take independent action for the acquisition of the Hayling Railway. He now offered on behalf of the LBSCR 'to admit the LSWR into a participation in the results of working the line'. In further discussion, the effect of the agreement for 'dividing the London and Isle of Wight railway traffic, having in view the independent access of the LSWR Company via Southampton', was touched upon and also the advantage of the Portsmouth route. If a proposed waterside extension was made to the Hayling line, which, however, the LBSCR did not intend to promote in any way, it was finally decided that the two companies should meet and come to terms for submission to the respective Boards regarding the competitive Isle of Wight traffic, including the course to be pursued in protecting the LSWR rights over the Hayling Railway.

The LSWR deputation was far from happy and a letter recapitulating the proceedings between the LBSCR, LSWR and Hayling Railway since 1864 was sent to the Brighton Directors, stating that the LSWR Board 'adhered to the protests already made against the course taken by the LBSCR in securing rental of the line'. The Brighton Directors 'abstained from the remarks on the retrospective position, in which they could not concur' and 'it was hoped the proposals made in the LBSCR Company's letter of 7th March would lead to a satisfactory arrangement of all questions between the two companies'. It was noted with satisfaction that by 1872 the Hayling Railway was out of the Receiver's hands as the local Directors had raised further funds and paid off outstanding debts to the contractor and other creditors.

On 30th October, 1872 Frank Whittaker suggested extending the Hayling Railway to the mouth of Langstone Harbour with a ferry thence across to Southsea, but in accordance with an agreement made with the LSWR, the LBSCR declined to participate. Then on 14th December, 1872 the Hayling Railway Board were advised that the LBSCR intended to postpone until the 1874 Parliamentary session any submission for a Bill including the agreement between the two companies, as the Brighton company had insufficient matters of importance to justify the expense of an application for a General Act in the 1873 session. The Hayling Railway, however, remained nominally independent until absorbed by the LBSCR in November 1922. Few alterations were initially made by the Brighton company save that the 'e' in Langstone was omitted from the station title from May 1873. Thus the railway became an integral part of the LBSCR branch line system offering a feeder service to the main line. Soon after transfer of operations the local company commenced paying a half-yearly dividend of 5 per cent on its £8,000 preference shares and a lesser amount on ordinary shares approximately every two years.

By powers granted by Act of Parliament, from 30th June, 1874 the Hayling company was leased to the LBSCR for a period of 1,000 years at an annual rental of £2,000 and establishment charges, which sufficed to pay the debenture interest and 5 per cent preference dividend regularly and dividends of between 2 and 2½ per cent on ordinary shares thereafter every two or three years. In the same year the Hayling company was embroiled in a lengthy disagreement with the South of England Oyster Co. over fishing rights. The impasse ended in court proceedings when the affair was settled in favour of both sides, with each claiming a pyrrhic victory. In the same year the company gave backing to the LBSCR to confer more rights to the main line company but the Bill was defeated. Then on 17th June, 1878 the LBSCR was granted powers by Act of Parliament to purchase the assets and works of the Hayling Bridge & Causeway Co., although no immediate effort was made to action the powers.

As the years evolved so minor improvements were made. In 1880 the original wooden station building at Langston was demolished and replaced by a larger timber structure, containing booking office and waiting room fronted over the platform by a small canopy. The LBSCR, however, could do little in combating the elements. During the great blizzard of 1881, the line was blocked for some days by deep snowdrifts. Two years later in September 1883, a severe south-westerly gale whipped up the relatively calm waters of Langstone Harbour until the line was flooded and the railway was closed to traffic for some days. Meanwhile in 1882 the LBSCR attempted to gain complete possession of both the Hayling Railway and the Woodside and South Croydon company in one Bill but the Hayling scheme was unsuccessful.

In 1885 Langston gained importance as the mainland link of a ferry service to the Isle of Wight. In that year the Isle of Wight Marine Transit Co. commenced a train ferry service from Langston to Brading Harbour, where a connection was made with Brading Harbour Railway & Works Co. at St Helen's Quay on the newly-opened Brading to Bembridge branch line, which was later worked by the Isle of Wight Railway. It was the first train ferry service to operate in the South of England and the only one ever to sail to the Isle of Wight. To operate the service a train ferry paddle steamer, the *Carrier*, was acquired from the North British Railway (NBR), where it had originally worked across the Firth of Tay between Tayport and Broughty Ferry.

The *Carrier*, an iron paddle steamer built by Scott Shipbuilding & Engineering Co. of Greenock Foundry, Greenock was launched on 16th November, 1858 and delivered to the railway company on 22nd November. She was 124 ft in length, 24 ft 7 in. wide, with draught of 5 ft 9 in., had a displacement of 243 tons and was capable of carrying 14 wagons. The vessel had two cylinders 42 inches in diameter with 36 inch stroke creating 112 horsepower operating a single crankshaft which was cheaper than the normal arrangement and this powered the independent paddle wheels. Curved plates covered the cranks. *Carrier* was a flat open deck vessel with two railway lines laid from bow to stern, one on the port side and one on the starboard, the rails being also laid close together, 4 ft 8½ in. apart so that wagons could be placed along the centre of the vessel using the two inner rails only. It had a funnel each side of the bridge, which spanned the centre of the vessel. Thomas Bouch, the Engineer and Manager of the Edinburgh & Northern Railway, and designer of the ill-fated first Tay Bridge, was mainly responsible for the design of the ship. The *Illustrated London News* of 16th February, 1859 called this type of vessel 'a floating railway'. *Carrier* operated across the Tay between Tayport and Broughty Ferry with a sister vessel the *Robert Napier* until the first Tay Bridge was built and opened in 1878. Earlier in the same year she was displaced by the PS *Midlothian*, which could carry 40 wagons, and was transferred with the *Robert Napier* to the Firth of Forth as a spare vessel on the Granton to Burntisland service. When the Tay Bridge collapsed in 1879 both vessels returned to the Firth of Tay where *Carrier* worked until 1882. In 1881 Samuel Lack Mason of Edinburgh, the General Manager of the North British Railway Company from 1867 until 1874, and later a Director of the NBR and also of the embryonic Isle of Wight Marine Transit Co., promoted the idea of a train ferry across the Solent between Langston and St Helens on the Isle of Wight. He subsequently purchased the *Carrier* in November 1881 for £3,400, the price including the moveable cradles and winding engines from Tayport and Broughty Ferry, and transferred them to the south of England in 1882.

Mason negotiated and subsequently entered into agreements with the LBSCR, the Receiver of the Brading Harbour Improvement & Railway Co., and other landowners to secure the rights to parts of the foreshore at Langston and at St Helens in Brading Harbour. The intention was to divert goods traffic from the mainland to the Isle of Wight via Havant, the Hayling Island branch to Langston, on the *Carrier* across the Solent to St Helens, and thence via the Isle of Wight Railway for onward delivery to island customers. It was thought the conveyance of goods by this route would obviate the need to load and unload at each ferry terminal, as was required via other crossings. The LBSCR entered into an agreement providing the traffic was not in competition with its existing arrangements with the LSWR on the Portsmouth to Ryde crossing. As the LBSCR and LSWR shared the facilities at Havant the former tried to encourage the latter into using the service but the LSWR declined to become involved.

A specification for the static equipment at Langston and St Helen's Quay indicated that the ramps, winding gear and engines were awaiting transport from Newhaven in 1883 and on 14th February, 1884 the Isle of Wight Marine Transit Co. was duly registered at Companies House, with an authorized share capital of £30,000 in 3,000 £10 shares. Jabez S. Balfour MP became Chairman and the finance came from a group of his companies, notably The Home & Land Investment Trust Co. (The Liberator Group). Balfour at the time was also Chairman of the Brading Harbour Improvement & Railway Co. with Henry S. Freeman as his deputy. The new transit company also agreed to purchase the benefits of the agreement previously made by Samuel Mason for £28,425, which included £7,000 for the *Carrier*, although part of the payment was in shares. When the company Prospectus was issued on 12th March, 1884 the first subscribers were William Drummond, solicitor of 21 Charlotte Square, Edinburgh; Alfred Burnie, solicitor, Adelaide Buildings, London Bridge, London EC; Francis Parry, Captain late 74th Highlanders, 4 Bank Buildings, London EC; Thomas Steill, merchant, 5 East India Avenue, London EC; Horatio Campbell Scott, bile broker, 1 St Michael's Alley, Cornhill,

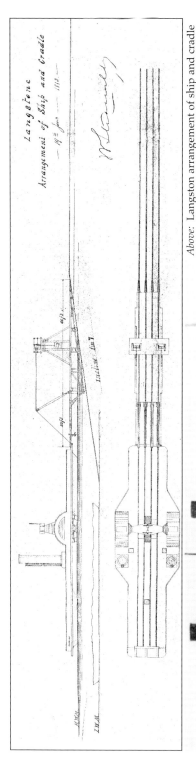

Above: Langston arrangement of ship and cradle for the *Carrier* ferry service to the Isle of Wight dated 19th June, 1883 and signed by William Stroudley.

Left: The train ferry *Carrier*, an iron paddle steamer built by Scott Shipbuilding and Engineering Co. of Greenock was launched on 16th November, 1858 and delivered to the North British Railway for service on the Firth of Tay between Tayport and Broughty Ferry. She was 124 ft in length, 24 ft 7 in. in width, had a displacement of 243 tons and could carry 14 wagons. The vessel was purchased by the Isle of Wight Marine Transit Co. and used from 1885 on the train ferry service between Langston and Brading harbour, which operated three times a week in each direction weather permitting. The LBSCR acquired the business but the venture was unsuccessful and the service was abandoned in March 1888. *Carrier* was laid up at Newhaven harbour and subsequently sold to a Swedish shipping line in May 1892 before being broken up the following year.

Author's Collection

London EC; John Gourdain Powers, merchant, Brixton Rise, Surrey and Edward Garthwaite Weaving, solicitor of 24 Coleman Street London EC. On 2nd July, 1884 *Carrier* was registered under the ownership of the Isle of Wight Transit Co.

By 3rd July, 1884, 1,207 shares had been issued but only £1 per share had been called. The chief shareholders were Stephen Clarke, coal factor, 4 St Dunstans Alley, London EC with 100 shares; John Perke Knight engineer, of Stafford House, Wickham, 100 shares; Samuel L. Mason, merchant of St Helens, West Coats, Edinburgh, 400 shares and Francis Parry, Managing Director of Railway Share Trust Co., 5 East India Avenue, London EC with 250 shares.

Work commenced converting the land on the western side of the single line Hayling Island branch at Langston, close by the northern end of the swing bridge, and also at St Helens at a point on the south quay on the harbour side of the Brading to Bembridge branch. Progress was slow and almost a year elapsed before completion could be envisaged. The *Isle of Wight County Press* on 20th June, 1885 reported:

> A great convenience is being arranged by the Joint Railway Companies, in the conveyance of goods from the mainland to the Island. They have purchased a vessel called the *Carrier*, to run between Langstone harbour and St Helens. The *Carrier* is open at each end, and has two sets of rails capable of holding fourteen trucks. Mr Scotter of the London and South Western Railway and Mr J P Knight of the London Brighton and South Coast Railway, have recently visited each port, and arrangements are being made so that the trucks will run from the main line into the boat and from the boat to the line at either end. The vessel is expected from Newhaven in a few days.

At the invitation of the Marine Transit Co. William Stroudley, Locomotive Engineer of the LBSCR and a number of other gentlemen visited the shore establishment at Langston to see at first hand the new arrangements.

On the morning of Saturday 4th July, 1885 the *Carrier* proudly sailed into Spithead, after thorough overhaul at Newhaven. The vessel was capable of accommodating seven trucks on each line of rails to a maximum of 140 tons of goods, in addition to the 56 tons tare weight of the wagons, thus allowing a loading of four tons per wagon. In practice it was thought advisable to have seven loaded wagons on one line and seven empty on the other. Loading and off-loading was from one end only, as there were buffer stops at the stern end. At the bow, a fix ramp allowed wagons to be rope hauled on and off the vessel. In the absence of any hinged link, the adaptor plates linked the track on the wharf to those on the vessel. When fully laden the *Carrier* was capable of travelling at between 7 and 8 knots and was able to make the 11 mile crossing, 4½ miles within the two harbours and 6½ miles in open water in 1½ hours, weather permitting. Skilful navigation was required within Langstone Harbour because of the extensive mud banks exposed at low tide, as well as the strong tidal flow. Before entering revenue earning service the *Carrier* made several test trips across the Solent and it was thought her annual working expenses would amount to between £1,400 and £1,600 and thus earn a handsome dividend for the transit company based on the existing traffic then passing between the mainland and the Isle of Wight.

The Marine Transit Company also entered an agreement with LBSCR to send Isle of Wight goods by the Langston to St Helens route for an agreed term of 21 years and to give the main line company the option to purchase the undertaking. The LBSCR however considered the LSWR should be given equal facilities if the undertaking were purchased, so as not to cause a monopoly. It was expected the service would stimulate the export of agricultural produce and livestock from the Island to the mainland and a number of other railway companies agreed to send their coal traffic to the Island at Portsmouth rates via the new route and the Marine Transit Company benefited accordingly. On 11th July, 1885 the *Isle of Wight County Press* reported that the London & North Western, the Midland, the Great Northern, the Great Western, the Great Eastern and the LBSC railway companies had agreed to send their coal traffic to the Isle of Wight via the new route at the Portsmouth rates.

By 5th August, 1885 the installations at both Langston and St Helens were completed and the new service was pronounced ready for opening from 6th August. It had originally been the intention to commence operations on 1st August but as the terminal works were not completed the service ultimately began on 1st September, 1885. *The Engineer* for 7th August, 1885 gave a detailed description of the working arrangements for loading and unloading of trucks at Langston. Railway tracks from the main single Hayling Island branch came up to the seaward end of the quay and rails were also laid on a timber jetty projecting down into the water, at an angle of 1 in 7 to a position approximately 4 ft below low tide level. A moving platform and a drawbridge, on 24 wheels with a flat section of decking with rails laid thereon would travel up and down the jetty, under the control of the drawing engine, in order to be at the same level as the stern of the PS *Carrier*, when she came into the docking position. When the rails on the deck of the vessel were aligned with the platform, drawbridge and quay there was a continuous line of rails with the added protection of a check-rail to prevent derailments. Ropes, which were already on the moving platform and drawbridge and attached to engines and winding gear on the quay, were then hooked on to coupling chains of the first wagon and the complete rake of wagons was then pulled on to the vessel. Loading was achieved by allowing the wagons to run on to the deck rails by gravity, checked and braked as necessary by the ropes attached to the coupling, and the winding drum on the quay. Loading and unloading was possible in quite a short space of time, depending on the state of the tide.

The service ran three times weekly in each direction, the major commodity conveyed in wagons on the ferry being coal and ballast dredged from Langstone Harbour. The *Carrier*, originally built for river and estuary sailings, experienced difficulties in adverse weather and choppy seas, especially on the exposed crossing of the Solent. As crossings were frequently cancelled at short notice, complaints started to mount and the expected traffic never materialized. The venture soon ran into financial difficulty and on 23rd December, 1885, the LBSCR entered into an agreement with the Marine Transit Co. for the hire of the *Carrier* and the use of the quays at each end of the route. Seven days later a resolution passed by the Marine Transit Co. agreed to increase the capital to £40,000. At a meeting on 7th September 1886, barely a year after the first service, it was agreed to wind up the affairs of the Marine Transit Co. and John Gourdain Powers was appointed liquidator with the remit to complete the sale to the LBSCR.

The *Isle of Wight Times* for 19th August, 1886 reported that the Marine Transit Co. had already disposed of the vessel and associated plant and wharves to the LBSCR for £40,000, although the sale was not completed until 24th November, 1886, and the final meeting of the transit company was held on 18th January, 1887. The LBSCR tried its best endeavours to make the service remunerative and at a meeting of the LBSCR shareholders the Chairman informed the gathering that the LSWR had proposed that the LBSCR should join with the LSWR in working the Southsea branch, whilst in return the LBSCR should allow the LSWR to work goods traffic from Havant to Langston and thence via the *Carrier* to St Helens.

To celebrate the 50th anniversary of accession to the throne by Queen Victoria, a Naval Fleet Review was held in Spithead on 22nd, 23rd and 24th July, 1887. The LBSCR spruced up the *Carrier* and used it to convey guests to review the ships. Unfortunately on one occasion *Carrier*, belching black smoke, sailed down the lines immediately in front of the Royal Yacht conveying Queen Victoria. Her Majesty and her entourage were not amused, and immediately afterwards the Lords Commissioners were careful to proscribe the review area to ordinary navigation.

Despite strenuous advertising by the LBSCR company, the combination of operating difficulties especially in adverse weather and moderate traffic returns forced abandonment of the service on 31st March, 1888, after which the *Carrier* was laid up at Newhaven to await further developments. None came and the vessel was subsequently sold to a Swedish shipping line in May 1892 and broken up in Sweden in 1893.

In the meantime a project, which might have had far reaching effects on the future of the Hayling line, was made in 1886 when authorization was given for an extension of the Southsea Railway, from its terminus thence across the entrance to Langstone Harbour to an end-on junction with the Hayling Island branch at South Hayling station. Had the plans succeeded the residential development of West Hayling might have accelerated, for the LBSCR proposed a circular train service via the Southsea branch, the new line, Hayling Island branch and then along the main line from Havant to Fratton. The bridge spanning the harbour mouth was proposed for use by both road and rail, and section 62 of the Act gave details of the proposed road toll. Economic difficulties were experienced, however, and the ambitious scheme fell into oblivion.

During a heavy thunderstorm on Monday 25th June, 1888, a man named Barnes employed by the LBSCR at Langston was struck by lightning and stunned which left him with temporary paralysis on one side. Arrangements were immediately made to convey him to his home at North Hayling, where he was attended by Doctor Norman.

The Regulation of Railways Act 1889, amongst other things, enforced railway companies to adopt block working on all single lines except where the Train Staff without Ticket and 'One Engine in Steam' systems existed. As the Hayling Railway was worked on the Train Staff and Ticket method of operation it was thus evident that the branch would have to be upgraded. In accordance with procedures the company was required to confirm to the BoT within two years the method to be adopted for working the branch. The Act also required the interlocking of points and signals at Havant, Langston, North Hayling and South Hayling. In the same year the LBSCR rebuilt the down or south side of Havant station by extending and re-roofing the station buildings and widening the platform. Havant Junction East signal box was re-sited from the east of the level crossing to the west side and a footbridge spanning the up and down main lines was provided to the east of the gates. Hayling Island branch services continued using the bay platform at the eastern end of the down platform. Additional sidings were installed for the interchange of branch traffic and the track layout was rearranged. The new work included interlocking of points and signals.

On Thursday 23rd January, 1890 a heavy westerly gale swept over the southern counties of England. Storms in the English Channel whipped up exceptionally high tides so that Langston swing bridge was submerged under the onslaught of wind and waves. Once the storm abated and the water receded it was found a portion of embankment near the bridge had been swept away in the onslaught resulting in the cancellation of train services for a few hours. A telegram from LBSCR headquarters to Portsmouth and distributed locally advised station masters and booking clerks not to issue any tickets to destinations on the South Hayling branch until further notice as traffic had been interrupted and repair were necessary. Fortunately the damage was not as severe as originally thought and repairs were made at a cost of £12. The branch was not as severely affected as further east along the coast where 430 yards of sea wall between Bishopstoke and Seaford was washed away necessitating considerable and costly repairs.

As the 2.05 pm Havant to South Hayling train was departing North Hayling on Wednesday 16th December, 1891, the engine and leading wheels of the first carriage derailed. The driver immediately applied the brakes and the train was brought to a stand within half its length. Some passengers walked on to South Hayling whilst others waited for road conveyance and no injuries were reported. Station master Mitchell of South Hayling quickly arranged road transport as a replacement service until the line was reopened two hours later. According to the *Hampshire Telegraph* the cause of the accident was attributed to the recent heavy rain and high tide, which had flooded part of the line undermining the ballast and sleepers which gave way under the weight of the locomotive.

At the end of the 19th century the LBSCR began a programme of improvements on the branch, initially renaming South Hayling station to Hayling Island from 1st June, 1892. Later in the year on 31st October the locomotive generally employed and outbased on the branch was returning from Portsmouth after repairs, initially running light engine to Havant manned by a Portsmouth driver and fireman, where it collected four wagons loaded with oysters from Whitstable and a brake van in which rode a porter. The continuing journey on the branch however, ended in disaster. It was the usual custom for the coaching stock forming the first up working to Havant to be stabled in the platform at Hayling Island and when the goods train approached the driver failed to apply the brakes in time and because of the slippery rails the engine collided with the empty carriages which were badly damaged as a result of the impact. The goods brake van also suffered fractured and bent buffers and the engine was slightly damaged. Station master Charles quickly assumed control of the situation and arranged for the engine to shunt the damaged stock to the siding before a train consisting of an undamaged third class coach and the brake van formed the 8.00 am up departure. Fortunately passengers had not joined the stock standing in the platform before the impact for had the collision occurred 20 minutes later a number of people would have sustained injury. Possibly as a result of the accident and with a view to reducing operating expenditure, it was subsequently found more economical to crew and maintain the branch locomotive at Portsmouth shed; the small engine shed at Hayling Island was closed and subsequently demolished in 1894. In the same year the up or north side of Havant station was rebuilt to handle increasing traffic handled at the junction, when additional sidings were laid in the goods yard on the north side of the line. At Hayling Island the booking office and ticket hall was enlarged in 1896 at a cost of £184 and two years later the siding formerly serving the engine shed was extended.

In the meantime on the afternoon of Thursday 29th August, 1895 a locomotive running round the Hayling Island train at Havant became derailed resulting in a delay to services for several hours. The *Hampshire Telegraph*, reporting the incident, remarked that it was the third time a locomotive had derailed within the space of 10 days! The permanent way staff were directed to investigate and make good any defective track to obviate future incidents.

At the North Hayling annual parish meeting held in late March 1899 the discussion opened with reference to the flooding of land and houses by high tides in Langstone Harbour near North Hayling station. W. Carpenter Turner reported that the council had been communicating with the LBSCR with the hope of inducing the company to raise the level of the railway or erect a sea wall alongside the permanent way. The company had replied that their Engineer would require to inspect the section of line before giving a decision. Turner said that failing this he would endeavour to get the company to provide or give permission for the council to place additional culverts for the water to pass under the railway so that the tidal water would return into the harbour instead of lying on the land for several days before drying out.

The *Hampshire Telegraph* for 1st April, 1899 reported that a deputation of local dignitaries had met with the LBSCR General Manager a few days earlier asking that provision be made for two trains to stand at Hayling Island station at the same time and for the provision of a canopy over the platform to provide protection for waiting passengers during inclement weather. There was no doubt the popularity of Hayling as a watering place had brought a considerable increase in traffic and the Brighton Directors heeded the request and duly authorized improvements. The deputation was also advised by the railway officers that the company planned to construct a larger goods shed at the terminal station because the increase in goods traffic.

From 1888 the landing gear and equipment used by the *Carrier* in the unsuccessful ferry service from Langston laid dormant at both Langston and St Helens. In 1900, an offer of £65 was made for redundant assets at St Helens but the LBSCR Board insisted on a payment of £75 before the material was removed. At Langstone, the harbour gradually silted up and sea trade was no longer viable and by 1900 most of the sidings had been altered.

Meanwhile after complaints regarding the branch train service the *Hampshire Telegraph* reported in May 1899 that the company was making some much needed alterations. From June 1899 a train would be arriving at Hayling Island at 7.45 am to form a 7.55 am return, specifically for businessmen, arriving at Havant at 8.15 am and connecting with onward services to Portsmouth, Brighton and London. The train conveying newspapers was retimed to arrive at Hayling Island at 9.15 am enabling residents to receive their paper some 45 minutes earlier. The 9.47 am up train ex-Hayling Island would depart at 9.37 am enabling passengers to connect with the London express departing Havant at 10.01 am. Another concession was that an evening train would connect with the theatre train at Havant on Thursdays between July and September to enable Hayling residents to attend Portsmouth theatres. The company also agreed to run a later train from Hayling Island to Havant at 8.10 pm but would not agree to a Sunday train service in the winter months. They had, however, entered into an agreement with the proprietor of the Grand Hotel to run a horse-drawn bus service on Sundays. It was also mentioned that the LBSCR was preparing plans for an extension to Hayling Island station and it had been agreed work on the two-sided platform was to commence forthwith. A goods shed was also to be erected.

A note in the *Weekly Express and Standard* for Saturday 22nd September, 1900 under the heading of 'Queer Travelling', advised readers that at North Hayling the train only stopped when the driver noted a passenger on the platform or if a passenger had advised the guard that he or she wished to alight - a fact already well known to regular travellers.

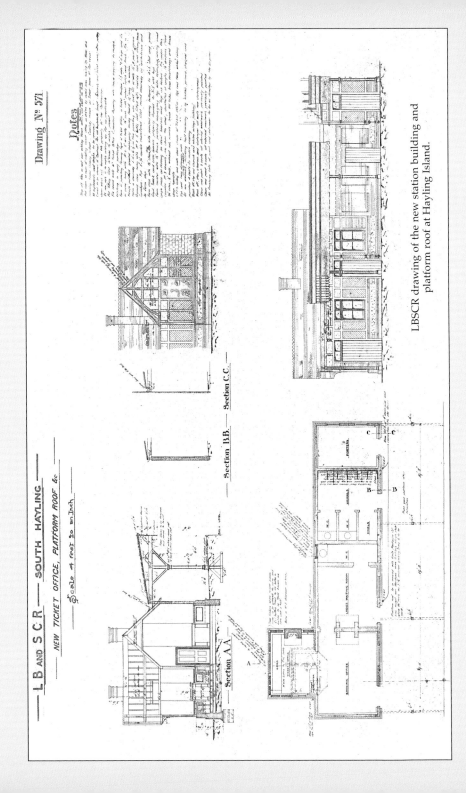

LBSCR drawing of the new station building and platform roof at Hayling Island.

To ease the operating difficulties experienced on the Hayling single line, with no passing places, a bay platform was duly installed on the west side of the platform at Hayling Island in 1900 served by the former engine shed siding which had been extended in 1898. Also in 1900 a new goods shed replaced the rather cramped wooden structure originally erected by the Hayling company and additional sidings were laid in the goods yard. Along the line at North Hayling, the LBSCR proposed a complete reconstruction of the station by doubling the length of the platform and the erection of a new and enlarged brick station building, to include general and ladies waiting rooms and ticket and parcels offices. The expected residential development in the catchment area of the station failed to materialize and the plans were later shelved. Two years later the canopy over the platform at Hayling Island was extended, whilst the rotting timbers of the original Langston bridge were renewed, the work being completed in 1903. The important work created some local interest for the *West Sussex Gazette* dated 5th May, 1904 erroneously advised its readers that the LBSCR authorities were to strengthen Langston swing bridge after the decision had been made to run main line trains to Hayling Island.

In 1906 the LBSCR authorities introduced a motor train service between Portsmouth and Chichester replacing normal locomotive-hauled stock with an 'A' class locomotive pulling stock in one direction and pushing on the return journey; later replaced by a 'D1' class 0-4-2 tank locomotive. With a view to rationalization of branch operating costs motor train working was also introduced between Havant and Hayling Island from January 1907 and the LBSCR Special Traffic Notice dated 26th January, 1907 advised staff of this, adding that the future passenger accommodation would be third class only. The new formation consisted of a class 'A1', later 'A1X' 0-6-0 tank locomotive and a 'Balloon' type driving brake third. One of the restrictions imposed by the introduction of the new service with its limited accommodation was that railwaymen were no longer allowed to purchase privilege tickets to ride on the branch, the exception being tickets issued from Hayling line stations for the staff of the Hayling branch. The local press were not enamoured with the introduction and the carriage of only third class passengers. 'It is claimed the service is to be improved but it may be pointed out that the most pressing need, that of a later train is quite ignored.' Further rationalization came later in the year when the original timber station building at North Hayling was found to be rotting away and was replaced by a simple wooden waiting shelter. Thereafter the station was unstaffed.

On 20th April, 1907 the *Hampshire Telegraph* reported that at a recent South Hayling Parish Council meeting a lengthy discussion took place with regard to the motor train service between Havant and Hayling Island, which was described as 'the most retrograde step ever undertaken on the island'. It was claimed it would seriously affect Hayling as a seaside resort. The chief objection was that half the single coach was set aside for smokers and that ladies and children were forced to go through the compartment to enter and leave the car. As the connection between the smoking and no-smoking section was being continually opened, the entire car was 'little better than a smoking compartment'. The coach also had insufficient luggage accommodation and frequently passengers placed parcels, trunks and cases down the central gangway blocking easy access to and from the doors. When the single coach was crowded with passengers the atmosphere was unpleasant, especially on the last train on a Saturday evening. One councillor reported he had made such a journey and 'was glad he did not have his wife and children with him'. The abolition of first and second class accommodation was having a 'bad effect on the better class of visitor to Hayling'.

Hayling Island station in the early 1900s soon after the track improvements and building of the goods shed. A three-coach train of Stroudley four-wheel coaches waits at the platform whilst the locomotive coaling stage can be seen between the run-round loop and the dock road, the end loading dock being in the foreground. Several wagons and a goods brake van stand on shed road.   *Author's Collection*

Hayling Island station in the early 1900s with a train of five LBSCR four-wheel coaches behind a 'Terrier' 0-6-0T pulling into the platform. The bay platform road is occupied by two four-wheel coaches. Note the difference in shading of the paintwork on the canopy frontage.
                                                                                 Author's Collection

'A1' class 0-6-0T No 663 *Preston* stands with the branch train formed of four-wheel Stroudley stock in the bay platform at Havant. By the time this photograph was taken the locomotive had been transferred to duplicate stock and received a wooden number plate on the bunker in place of the original brass No. 63. She retained her name for a short period before even that was taken away. *O.J. Morris*

'A1' class No. 78 *Knowle* stands at the head of a typical Hayling Island branch train at Langston around the turn of the century. The locomotive retains its copper-capped chimney and appears to have burnished buffers. In true branch line tradition the locomotive carried a route indicator disc as well as a headlamp. *Knowle* was later transferred to duplicate stock and renumbered 678. The SR transferred her to the Isle of Wight in May 1929, becoming No. W4 and then W14 receiving the name *Bembridge*, where she remained before transferring back to the mainland in May 1936 as No. 2678. *Author's Collection*

The arrival of the branch train at Hayling Island in the early 1900s has provided custom for at least one of the horse-drawn conveyances waiting in the approach road. The railway company planted the trees to provide a windbreak against the prevailing south-west wind at this exposed location. *Author's Collection*

With the Havant Junction starting signal cleared for the Guildford route, LSWR class 'K10' 4-4-0 No. 386 departs with an up main line service to Waterloo as an LSWR class 'T1' 0-4-4T busies itself shunting the goods yard. The Hayling Island branch bay platform to the left is occupied by a rake of Stroudley four-wheel coaches. *Author's Collection*

Bookings for first and second class were not available at Hayling Island or the other branch stations and passengers had to book third class to Havant and rebook first or second class from there for their forward journey.

The railway authorities realized the strength of feeling against the rail motor service and the detrimental effect it might have on patronage and traffic if it continued during the summer months. Accordingly normal locomotive haulage was re-introduced during the period June to September with the motor train service resuming for the autumn. The *Hampshire Telegraph* thus reported on 5th October, 1907 that 'the LBSC Railway Company have resumed motor train services on the Havant to Hayling Island line but have as a concession decided to retain the late train through October.' It added as a rider that if the late train was well supported it would continue through the winter months.

After Germany declared war on France and Belgium, Britain declared war on Germany on 4th August, 1914 and within days, volunteers for the armed forces were departing from Hayling Island and the other branch stations. The departures by train were proud but sad occasions as some did not return. On the outbreak of World War I, the LBSCR with other British railway companies came under Government control from the same date, under the powers of Section 16 of the Regulation of the Forces Act 1871 with the Railway Executive Committee taking control under the chairmanship of Herbert Walker, later Sir Herbert Walker, of the LSWR. The Hayling Island branch services initially continued to run to pre-war timetables but the issue of all excursion and cheap day tickets was suspended and all competition between companies cancelled. Goods traffic increased as additional produce from local farms was sent to towns and cities to make up for the loss of imported goods. Even hay was cut from the railway embankments and sent to military stables. Some local railwaymen also quickly answered the call to arms and joined the colours in the first few months of hostilities. Not all was doom and gloom for in 1915 there was a boom in first class travel on the LBSCR as many travellers who usually migrated to France or Switzerland took their holidays at south coast resorts, including Hayling Island.

By December 1916 the strain of the war effort was taxing the resources of all British railways to such an extent that the Railway Executive issued an ultimatum that they could only continue if drastic reductions were made to ordinary and non-essential services. The Lloyd George Coalition Government agreed to a reduction in passenger services from 1st January, 1917, but with these economic measures the Hayling Island branch lost only one train in each direction as many services were operated as mixed trains conveying goods. Thus the branch continued its useful activity giving regular passenger, freight and parcels services to the local community. In the same month further evidence of railway encouragement to local people came after Germany's 'sink at sight' submarine campaign threatened imports of food and near starvation. Allotment holders, including those with plots alongside the branch, were encouraged to increase cultivation of vegetable and fruit and the LBSCR management produced a guide for allotment holders and an assortment of 43 pamphlets as well as advice by poster.

During the night of Thursday 23rd August, 1917 a fire was discovered on Langston railway bridge but before it could be quelled several of the timbers were destroyed and damage was so severe that railway services were suspended. The accident was believed accidental, possibly caused by stray sparks emanating from the engine of the last up train to cross the bridge the previous evening. Repairs, however, were soon effected and services returned to normal.

At the turn of the century the LBSCR management were concerned about operating losses and introduced auto-train working. From January 1907 most of the Hayling Island branch services were converted to motor train working with the 'A1' or 'A1X' class 0-6-0T hauling a 'Balloon' coach or coaches dating from 1905-07 but despite being unpopular the method of working continued until 1916. Here 'A1' class No 663 *Preston* stands in the up platform at Havant station with a main line motor train working from Portsmouth in the first decade of the 20th century. Behind the train can be seen Havant West signal box and Leigh Road level crossing.

Author's Collection

'Terrier' 0-6-0T No B661 standing at Hayling Island station with her two-coach train from Havant in the early 1920s. The locomotive is working Fratton duty No. 376 as denoted on the route indicator disc and is preparing to run-round the stock. A Nestle's vending machine for chocolates occupies a position by one of the platform stanchions.   *Author's Collection*

The general feeling of elation felt by the cessation of hostilities in November 1918 was shattered by a railway strike, which halted branch services from 26th September to 5th October, 1919. The action undermined the patronage enjoyed by the railway as prospective passengers sought alternative modes of transport. Serious inroads were being made into the monopoly enjoyed by the LBSCR as a local bus service had been introduced between Havant and Hayling Island. The industrial unrest began the slow decline in the meagre freight services. Farmers and growers realised for the first time that with improving roads, goods could be conveyed by lorry, using in some cases vehicles purchased second-hand from the military. Thus short journeys to and from Portsmouth and Chichester and other local markets were possible at rates cheaper than charged by the LBSCR. The door-to-door services were more convenient than the double handling into and out of railway wagons. The primitive road vehicles of the day were not, however, capable of continuous long hauls, and middle and long distance traffic remained safely in the hands of the railway company. Although peace had been declared the Government retained control of the railways until 15th August, 1921 as the war effort had seriously debilitated the concerns with little or minimal maintenance of rolling stock and infrastructure. In 1918 the Coalition Government had hinted at support for nationalization, a thought that had been festering since the formation of the Railway Nationalisation League in 1895 and with later support of the railway unions and the formation of the Railway Nationalisation Society in 1908. A number of industrialists and traders were sympathetic saying the railways should be a public corporation rather than a profit making concern. In the event the government fell short of full nationalization and formed the companies into four groups. Thomas Eggar, a London lawyer, was Chairman of the Hayling Railway Board prior to Grouping.

LBSCR 'A1X' class 0-6-0T No. 655 formerly No. 55 *Stepney* runs round the branch train at Havant in the early 1920s. A spare set of four-wheel coaching stock stands in the back siding whilst an open wagon with tarpaulin sheet occupies the middle road. Note the ornate lighting columns and distinctive station buildings. *Stepney* was later to gain fame in preservation on the Bluebell Railway. *Author's Collection*

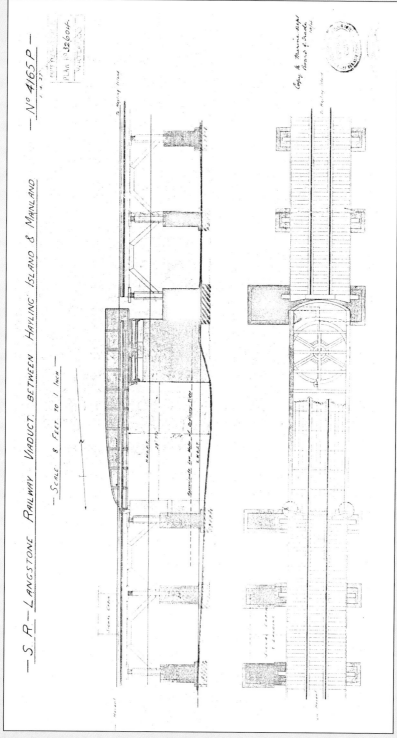

SR diagram of Langston railway viaduct showing the concrete bases to the bridge supports, dated 4th April, 1927.

Chapter Three

Southern Railway Ownership

As a result of the 1921 Railways Act, from 1st January, 1923, the LBSCR was amalgamated with the London and South Western, South Eastern and Chatham and several smaller railway companies to form the Southern Railway. The Hayling Railway, whilst remaining nominally independent of the LBSCR until November 1922, was absorbed to become a minor branch line of the new company.

The new regime made few initial changes to the branch but as the months passed the Brighton livery on the locomotives gave way to Southern Railway green whilst the coaching stock followed suit, although ex-LSWR stock quickly replaced most of the former LBSCR vehicles on the branch. Industrial action affected affairs and a seven-day rail strike from 20th January, 1924 brought a decline in traffic. The deteriorating relationship between trades unions and the railway company only served to encourage competition and gradually bus services offering almost door-to-door services appeared, although still restricted by the vehicle weight limits on Langstone road bridge. The affairs of the branch were again disrupted by the General Strike in early May 1926. Railway union members withdrew their labour in support of the miners' and subsequently train services could not be guaranteed. On several days the Hayling Island services were suspended. Fortunately within a week regular railwaymen returned to duty and services resumed. The impact of the continuing miners strike meant reduced coal stocks available to the railway companies and the SR authorities decided on the only course of action available to conserve stocks by reducing train services for a short period.

The relationship between the railway company and the unions was not the only problem for management as competitive bus services continued to increase in frequency. However, even they were not finding progress easy for, early in 1926, South Hayling Parish Council complained to Havant Urban Council of the poor motor bus services. The matter was raised with Mr Holt the General Manager of the bus company who advised the council that the two existing bus companies were being reorganized and merged under one management. He then indirectly criticized the local authorities, stressing that the chief problem was the bad roads on the island and as many as four springs were being fractured on vehicles every day! Because of the condition of the roads it was not the intention to introduce more modern buses on the island until matters improved. Holt added that the SR authorities had shown open hostility against the bus services and it was his opinion the bus companies did not get the support that they should.

The SR also came in for criticism in February 1926 when the *Hampshire Telegraph* reported that after innumerable delays Portsmouth Corporation Electric Co. had at last extended supplies to Hayling Island with the Royal Hotel the first building to receive the new electric lighting. A considerable number of houses on the island had also been wired for supply for two years but the difficulties had resulted from the reluctance of the railway company to grant wayleaves for cable routes from the mainland at Langstone crossing SR property and the road and railway bridges.

Before Grouping the LBSCR Engineer had been grappling with the deteriorating condition of Langston viaduct and the new regime decided major modification work was necessary if the line was not to close. Surveys were conducted and it was decided to renew bridge timbers and encase them in concrete from above high water

'A1X' class 0-6-0 No. 653, not yet painted and renumbered by its new owner, stands at Langston with a down train on 3rd October, 1925. The locomotive was formerly LBSCR No. 53 *Ashstead* and was subsequently sold to the Weston, Clevedon & Portishead Railway in February 1937, becoming that railway's No. 4. The Somerset undertaking was taken over by the Great Western Railway in 1940 and the locomotive was withdrawn in 1948. *Author's Collection*

A fine study of 'A1X' class 0-6-0T No. B662 at Langston in the 1920s. The locomotive was originally LBSCR No. 62 *Martello* and was a regular performer on the Hayling Island branch until withdrawal from traffic in November 1963. The locomotive has been preserved. *Author's Collection*

mark to the bed of the creek. Work commenced in the spring of 1926 and proceeded quite slowly hampered by the tidal waters and inclement weather. Some existing timbers were retained but the original 19 ft gap between piers was reduced to 18 feet as additional cladding was attached for strengthening. The uprights were then encased in concrete. Unfortunately an inspection on 2nd September, 1926 revealed that in several cases vertical cracks had been recorded in the piers already completed due to vibration to the timber superstructure caused by trains passing over the structure. It was decided to add additional reinforcement bars with one inch diameter by 13 ft steel insert rods. This hampered the work, which was not finally completed until 1931. The SR made few other changes, although by the early 1930s passenger services over the branch had increased in number to cope with the popularity of Hayling Island as a holiday resort. A minor thorn in the side of the railway company was the increasing number of private cars and public service vehicles. During these years considerable holiday and private development was made on Hayling but, except for small pockets near North Hayling Halt and Hayling Island station, most expansion tended to be near or adjacent to the main road and to the east and south-east of the island, away from the line.

On several occasions between 1934 and 1939 during the summer months deprived children from London's east end were brought to Hayling Island to spend a day by the sea. The trains, usually formed of non-corridor SR stock, were hauled to and from Havant by a main line locomotives and then worked over the branch by a 'Terrier' tank locomotive sent especially from Fratton shed, leaving the locomotive allocated to the branch to maintain the normal services. The stock was stabled in the goods yard after the children had alighted and before the return working, with local staff carrying out internal cleaning. It must be assumed that toilet stops were made on both the down and up main line journeys.

A vital increase in the use of the branch came in July 1937 and 1938 after the electrification of the main line from Waterloo to Portsmouth and coastal line from Brighton to Portsmouth. With the rapid interval services to coastal towns and London, Hayling further increased in popularity with holidaymakers and passenger services were again improved to cope with the demand.

The rebuilding of Havant station in 1937 and 1938 at the time of the electrification, involved the station site being relocated further west. The old station was demolished and the new northern or up side platform was set further back to leave room for a four-track layout, the centre roads being for through traffic. An overbridge replaced the level crossing at the western end of the station, whilst two signal boxes, Havant West and Havant North, the latter on the former LSWR line, were abolished on 1st May, 1938 and 3rd November, 1935 respectively. Havant Junction signal box, plain Havant from 1st May, 1938, which also controlled the Hayling Island branch traffic, was retained and the equipment modernized, and colour light signalling installed on the main lines only. The new station, built in modern 'Odeon' style, was completed in white concrete with metal window frames. Whilst these improvements were carried out the Hayling Island branch services used a temporary wooden platform aligned to the former run-round loop. On completion the branch traffic utilized the bay at the back of the former and now much extended down platform, which was devoid of shelter and further from the new booking office.

Just prior to the outbreak of World War II on 1st September, 1939, the SR with all other railway companies came under the control of the Railway Executive Committee. Within weeks of the commencement of hostilities local bus services were

In early SR days 'A1X' class 0-6-0T No. B655 curves away from Langston with the 9.20 am ex-Havant mixed train om 29th July, 1931 formed of ex-LSWR non-gangway brake composite and brake third, five open wagons and an ex-LBSCR goods brake van.   *Author's Collection*

The 9.30 am Havant to Hayling Island mixed train approaches Langston bridge behind 'A1X' class No. B655 on 25th May, 1932. The eight wagons and brake van at the rear of the ex-LSWR short wheelbase bogie coaches include three LMS, one GWR, one SR and three private owner open wagons demonstrating healthy freight revenue for the branch at this time.   *O.J. Morris*

In 1901 the LBSCR purchased a Wallis & Stevens steam roller for levelling the surface of goods yards and roadways. The vehicle painted umber and fitted with a copper-capped chimney is shown in Hayling Island goods yard in 1933.   *O.J. Morris*

'Terrier' No. 2653 awaits in Havant bay platform ready to depart for Hayling Island in the early 1930s. The connection under the locomotive and added in 1899 was probably required for the transfer of vehicles to and from main line services.   *Dr I.C. Allen*

Havant station facing east during the alterations of 1937-38. The old LBSCR station buildings are being demolished to make way for the provision of four tracks. During this period a temporary wooden platform was provided for Hayling Island branch services pending the completion of a new bay and track alterations.   *Author's Collection*

After the rebuilding of Havant station in 1937/8 'A1X' class 0-6-0T No. 2661 stands at the new bay platform waiting to depart for Hayling Island. The locomotive is in fully lined-out livery, evident on the front of the side tank and cab and carried Fratton depot duty No. 375 on the headcode disc.   *Author's Collection*

reduced and some removed from the road by petrol rationing, which came into effect on 16th September. The island was expected to suffer aerial bombardment as the branch was on the south coast and adjacent to the naval port of Portsmouth and a number of schemes including blackout and air raid precautions were introduced. In order to safeguard against air raids and possible land invasion especially at night, the station lamps remained dimmed, and staff utilized shielded hand lamps to attend to train or shunting duties. Posts and other obstacles on station platforms received white stripes of paint to obviate people walking into them in the dark or blackout. As a precaution against enemy attacks station nameboards were initially removed and stored in lamp rooms or signal boxes, but were later reinstated. The agricultural nature of freight handled on the branch was again of the utmost importance as vital provisions of home-grown food, grain and vegetables were dispatched and conveyed to local markets.

During World War II, services were barely reduced and being in a restricted and strategic military area, many service personnel were conveyed on the branch. From 1939 an unadvertised later train worked from Havant to Hayling Island calling at the intermediate stations returning off duty military personnel back to their camp after an evening out in Havant or Portsmouth. It was claimed the running of the special obviated inebriated sqaddies from upsetting local civilian passengers. As predicted the close proximity of Portsmouth, which was a prime target for marauding Luftwaffe aircraft, meant that the branch was in constant danger from air attack but fortunately except for a few near misses in Langstone Harbour, the line remained virtually unscathed. For railwaymen working the branch services at this time one of the most difficult duties was to locate North Hayling Halt at night, for with total blackout the station was hard to position, and drivers and guards frequently had to resort to counting telegraph poles from Langston bridge as a guide. As part of the defence of the area, anti-aircraft heavy batteries were based on Hayling Island in the war, but the road bridge was too weak to carry the turret guns. These were brought to Langston, loaded on to flat wagons and taken by rail on to the island. One of the anti-aircraft batteries equipped with heavy $5\frac{1}{2}$ inch guns was located near North Hayling Halt. Another was sited a short distance east of the railway mid-way between North Hayling and Hayling Island. On 10th/11th January, 1941 the Luftwaffe with 153 bombers carried out a devastating attack on Portsmouth in which 171 persons were killed. Some of the bombs landed in Langstone Harbour but the branch remained unscathed. To protect Portsmouth from German night bombing decoy sites were built in Langstone Harbour and on Sinah Common. Hayling Island. The experiment met with some success for on 17th/18th April, 1941, 140 aircraft were lured away from the city and unloaded in excess of 200 incendiaries and bombs into Langstone Harbour and Farlington Marshes, again with no damage to the branch line.

During hostilities a considerable number of allied aircraft crashed on Hayling Island including a Blenheim fighter, which ditched near the railway at North Hayling on 21st June, 1941. Because of weight restrictions on the road bridge a considerable tonnage of metal and other debris from damaged aircraft was loaded on to rail wagons at Hayling Island for conveyance to the mainland. The establishment of three Royal Navy training bases on Hayling Island known as Northney I, II and III resulted in many personnel travelling across the branch at the commencement and termination of their courses and exercises. The up side sidings at Langston saw little use in the 1930s and during the early war years and having assumed a state of dereliction were lifted in 1944.

After the war the railways resumed peacetime activities with run-down and life-expired rolling stock and equipment, and infrastructure in need of maintenance. Questions were raised in Parliament regarding the deteriorating services offered and the Hayling Island branch was no exception. The summer of 1946 was the first opportunity for families to take holidays since before the war and many services were crowded with day trippers as well as those spending a week by the sea, despite fares rising by 16 per cent from pre-war levels. The severe weather early in 1947 also brought problems, initially with drifting snow blocking cuttings and then rapidly thawing snow causing minor flooding. Damage was so severe that permanent way staff had to replace waterlogged sleepers and replace ballast. Mother nature was not the only problem for, as petrol rationing eased, so Southdown Motor Services improved the frequency on local bus routes. Further progress was hampered by a critical shortage of coal supplies and the Government announced at the end of April 1947 that to conserve stocks for the following winter, train services were to be cut by 16 per cent compared with the summer of 1946.

Optimistically for the SR management after the hostilities there was a gradual revival of holiday traffic and train services, although not up to pre-war levels, increased to handle the influx of passengers, especially during the summer months. The length of some trains on summer Saturdays required a turnover engine at both Havant and Hayling Island to maintain the frequent service and necessitated the use of three locomotives. Thus the outlook for the branch line was brighter as nationalization of the railways approached.

SR 'Terrier' 0-6-0T No. 2635 spins along the branch between Havant and Langston in the late 1930s with a down train. The locomotive carries a copper-capped chimney and displays Fratton duty No. 376 on the head disc.   *C.R.L. Coles*

Chapter Four

Nationalization and Closure

The nationalization of the railways from 1st January, 1948, brought few changes to the Hayling Island line, which to many appeared in a time warp with LBSCR locomotives and LBSCR-, LSWR- or early SR-designed coaching vehicles. Most stocks of SR tickets were quickly used up especially those in constant demand, which were replaced by those bearing the legend 'Railway Executive' or 'British Railways'. Locomotives working the line gradually lost the 'Southern' on the side tanks to be replaced by the austere 'British Railways' and later the lion and wheel emblem. The livery also changed from SR green to lined black. Coaching stock remained various shades of green depending on their last visit to the shops but later some received a crimson red livery. British Railways (Southern Region) initially made few alterations to timetables but as holiday traffic continued to grow, changes were made during the summer months to cater for increasing numbers travelling to the holiday camps established on the island. However, as petrol rationing eased the renewed onslaught of the emerging privately owned motor car with the convenience of door-to-door service and the competitive Southdown buses using single-deck Leyland 'Tiger' vehicles serving the centres of population on the island cast a shadow over the line. Whilst summer passenger totals continued to increase the winter numbers of local railway passengers declined and often trains ran with only one coach. The railway, however, retained its advantage over road for passengers travelling on the Southdown service 47 to Havant, later employing 30-seater Dennis Falcon buses, had to alight before it crossed the road bridge and then rejoin the vehicle because of continuing weight restrictions. Some traffic was lost in the summer months to Southdown service 149 worked by open top Guy 'Arab' buses, which passed Hayling Island station and served the ferry link to Portsmouth.

In April 1951 'Terrier' 0-6-0 tank locomotive No. 2647, still in Southern Railway livery, which had spent some 25 years at Newhaven, where its annual mileage and hence shopping interval was insignificant, was transferred to Fratton in order to get its mileage up on the Hayling Island branch. However, whilst working a service train it disgraced itself by fracturing a crank axle near Langston bridge and blocked the line. The engine was eventually removed to Langston siding and on the following Sunday it was towed to Havant station, where with the aid of Fratton breakdown crane No. DS81 lifting the locomotive, the offending wheel set was removed. The engine was then hauled to Fratton shed for remedial attention. At the turn of the year rumours abounded concerning the possible closure of the line.

On Saturday 9th February, 1952 the inhabitants of Havant were invited to air their views in the BBC programme *Speak Your Mind*. When asked as to what people thought about the possible closure of the Havant to Hayling Island branch line a Mrs Elliott of Hayling Island proffered some comments. The good lady questioned why cheap day tickets were available from Havant to Hayling Island but not from Hayling Island to Havant, where residents were forced to purchase monthly return tickets. She was also scathing on the filthy conditions of the branch trains saying she always felt the need to take along a vacuum cleaner to clean the compartment before entering and a chamois leather to clean the windows so she could enjoy the view!

As road transport went from strength to strength so freight traffic, which had only been a minor factor in the branch finances, steadily transferred to road haulage, leaving just

'A1X' class 0-6-0T No. 32662 departing from Havant with the 3.35 pm to Hayling Island on 13th September, 1953. The train is passing over New Lane level crossing and in the background is Havant signal box and beyond that the railway cottage on the opposite of the main line. Note that the locomotive is carrying the incorrect route headcode for the branch. *Author's Collection*

'A1X' class 0-6-0T No. 32650 waits hopefully for passengers in the branch platform at Havant before working the 1.35 pm to Hayling Island on 12th May, 1956. To the left of the train is the run-round loop and next to that, Leggett's siding. Sister locomotive No. 32640, which has worked the inward branch service, stands by the buffer stops. *R. Buckley*

coal and coke and heavier items handled by rail. The final straw came with the opening of the new road bridge connecting Langstone with Hayling at noon on 10th September, 1956 replacing the original wooden structure, which was life-expired. The Rt Hon. A.H.E. Molson, Parliamentary Secretary to the Minister of Transport, officially opened the new structure using a solid gold key. At the time it was the biggest venture in Hampshire since World War II and was considered an outstanding example of pre-stressed concrete designed by the County Surveyor, Brigadier A.C. Hughes. The beams and piles had been pre-cast in Langstone Quay car park, which had been levelled, and an on-site laboratory was built to test the materials. The beams were taken out to the bridge on a small narrow gauge railway, the wagons being hauled by a small diesel locomotive. The piles were then rammed into place using a 100 tons capacity pile driver. The contractor Christiani & Neilson completed the project five months ahead of schedule at an estimated cost of £311,000. At the opening ceremony the Assistant Bishop of Portsmouth blessed the bridge and the first vehicle to cross was a horse-drawn black and yellow coach driven by Sir Dymoke White, the Vice Chairman of Hampshire County Council. The dignitaries later lunched at Warblington Secondary School where senior girls served the meals. At 3.50 pm the contractor drove the first car across the bridge and soon after a double-deck bus passed over, marking the start of a through service from Havant station to Hayling Island in direct competition to the railway. Ironically the first pedestrian to cross the bridge and pay the 1*d*. toll was E. Edwards, station master at Havant. Demolition of the old structure commenced on 11th September. The new bridge retained its status as a toll bridge for only a few years, for *The Times* of 11th April, 1960 carried a photograph of a British Railways, Southern Region employee, with the caption, 'At four o'clock this afternoon the Langstone Bridge, which links Hayling Island with the mainland, will be freed from tolls by the Hampshire County Council. Yesterday Mr Clarke was receiving some of the last tolls to be paid'. The Southdown bus services to and from Havant were immediately transformed when the company introduced Guy 'Arab' and Leyland 'PD' and 'TD' vehicles on the route, bringing a steady decline in rail travel as passengers were spared the former ritual of walking across the bridge. (The heaviest vehicle allowed on the old timber road bridge was 6 tons 6 cwt, further reduced to 5 tons in 1954.)

Although one barrier was removed from the free access to Hayling Island Langston level crossing still caused considerable congestion at summer weekends, especially with the enhanced train services. The three holiday camps which had developed on the island continued to attract clientele travelling by rail and a half-hourly interval service was again operated on summer Saturdays and Sundays. Day-trippers from the rapidly growing areas of Portsmouth, Gosport and Fareham, as well as London and the metropolis swelled passenger numbers. These special summer services required the use of three locomotives, so that there was always a turnover engine at each end of the line. On these days the coal stage at Hayling Island and locomotive coal wagon beside the run-round loop and watering facilities at Havant were constantly used as the 'Terrier' tank locomotives had a limited water and bunker capacity, and needed regular replenishment.

By the early 1960s, however, it was realised that both rolling stock and the fixed assets of the branch were deteriorating rapidly. Closure of the Hayling Island branch, originally mooted in the early 1950s was resurrected in September 1962, with complete closure advocated from 31st December, 1962. Unlike many threatened branch lines revenue on the Hayling Island line covered operating costs and in 1961 a profit of £2,000 was made. However, the great emphasis and dependence on holiday traffic meant the line was heavily used in the few summer months with little traffic in the winter as ascertained from the following passenger statistics from Hayling Island station for winter and summer of 1961.

Hayling Island station facing the buffer stops with 'A1X' class 0-6-0T No. 32640 standing at the main platform with the 12.55 pm train for Havant on 12th May, 1956. The bay platform is occupied by stabled coaching stock. Permanent way replacement is evidently in hand for sleepers are heaped between the run-round loop and the dock road siding, whilst replacement rails lie alongside the main platform road. Away from the canopy the platform surface is of crushed gravel.   *Author's Collection*

On a damp and misty 24th March, 1957 a Locomotive Club of Great Britain railtour train visited the Hayling Island branch. 'Terrier' 0-6-0Ts Nos. 32636 without spark arrester and No. 32650 with spark arrester stand in the down main platform at Havant before setting off down the branch. Because of weight restriction on the branch No. 32636 was detached and then attached to the rear of the train before starting the journey. Note the ex-LNER buffet car included in the six-coach train.   *V.R. Webster/Kidderminster Railway Museum*

| *Tickets collected* | March | 2,077 | August | 32,176 |
| *Tickets issued* | March | 1,705 | August | 7,019 |

The factor, which weighed heavily against retention of the line in the future railway network, was the replacement of the infrastructure. By early 1962 it was realised an expenditure of £400,000 would be required to rebuild Langston viaduct if traffic was to be carried at all, and certainly to accommodate larger and heavier locomotives than the life-expired 'Terrier' tank locomotives. As the revenue from the branch did not cover even the interest payable on such an investment, the result was inevitable and the usual closure notices were posted.

Despite such threats the Southern Region *Holiday Haunts* booklet for 1962 still enthused,

Hayling Island is becoming more and more popular both with those who delight in a quiet and informal holiday and with those who enjoy the equally informal, yet rather more robust delights of the holiday camp. There are sun and safe sea bathing on the five-mile sandy shores with plenty of open-air recreation, including boating and angling. There is an 18 hole golf course near the beach, and at Rowland's Castle and Waterlooville courses are within easy reach.

Unfortunately there was no effort to encourage rail travel between Havant and Hayling Island.

Objections to the closure of the branch were quickly made known, and the Urban District Council of Havant and Waterloo, Hayling Island Chamber of Trade, Hayling Island Residents' Association, Havant and Bedhampton Electors and Ratepayers Association, Portsmouth Trades Council and 49 other objectors made representations. The necessary Transport Users' Consultative Committee hearing was held in Havant Town Hall on 12th December, 1962 but the case of the rickety bridge and ageing rolling stock won the day. Despite arguments against the shortcomings of the existing bus services, the TUCC after deliberating the evidence for and against, advised the Minister of Transport that closure of the line could be effected provided the bus services were augmented. The application to the Traffic Commissioner and the additional licences for Southdown bus services took some time to complete and the branch was reprieved for the summer of 1963, although the infamous Beeching Report of the same year only reiterated the proposal. Permission was finally granted to withdraw the passenger and freight rail services on and from Monday 4th November, 1963, but as there were no winter Sunday services, the last public passenger trains ran on Saturday 2nd November, 1963. One of the conditions of closure was the holding of a six-month trial to see if the alternative bus services operated by Southdown were suitable; a luggage-in-advance service had to continue between Havant and Hayling Island and BR officials had to keep themselves informed and inform the Minister of any proposals to alter the substitute bus services. It was claimed Hayling Island, as with other south coast resorts, had a concentrated season during the summer months but very little traffic in the winter and with these variations any trial held between November and May would be tantamount to cheating. Having made the decision no such trial was conducted.

For the final day of public working, Saturday 2nd November, 1963, trains were strengthened to three coaches and a special augmented service operated at 30 minute intervals after the 2.20 pm departure from Havant for the remainder of the afternoon and evening to cater for the many local passengers and railway enthusiasts who wished to ride on the 'Hayling Billy' for the last time. 'Terrier' tank locomotives Nos. 32650, 32662 and 32670 were rostered to work turn and turn about during the day. All the

On the approach to Hayling Island station the branch turned slightly inland away from the waters of Langstone Harbour and here No. 32650 with a down train climbs the 1 in 321 gradient on the last lap of its journey from Havant on 29th October, 1962.   *Ken Paye*

With steam up 'Terrier' 0-6-0T No. 32650 stands in the bay platform at Havant on 29th October, 1962 as driver and guard exchange pleasantries.   *Ken Paye*

Hayling Island station and goods yard view facing south in November 1962 with 'A1X' class 0-6-0T No. 32650 running round her train. To the left the land beside the back road is being used as storage grounds by local coal merchants, whilst the brake van and other wagons stand on the shed road. *Author*

The diminutive size of the 'Terrier' tank locomotives made for easy arranging of coal supplies in the bunker. Here the fireman carries out the duty with ease from the platform at Hayling Island on No. 32650 as she stands at the head of the 5.06 pm to Havant in November 1962. The run-round loop is to the left. *Author*

The last day of operation on the Hayling Island branch as 'A1X' No. 32670 stands at the rear of the five-coach LCGB 'Hayling Farewell Rail Tour' train at Havant prior to working the special to Hayling Island on 3rd November, 1963. *Author*

General view of the scene at Hayling Island on the afternoon of Sunday 3rd November, 1963 before departure of the LCGB 'Hayling Farewell Rail Tour' behind 'A1X' class No. 32670 assisted in the rear by No. 32636. Minutes after this view was taken the train had left for Havant, the station site became deserted and the branch was officially closed the following day. *Author*

remaining goods wagons were cleared from Hayling Island by the 7.54 pm up departure to Havant and the last down passenger service 8.39 pm ex-Havant departed some 20 minutes late behind 'Terrier' No. 32662. For the final public up service 9.00 pm ex-Hayling Island, a locomotive was coupled fore and aft of the six-coach train with No. 32650 at the head and No. 32662 at the rear. With laurel wreath and headboard attached to the smokebox door of the leading engine, the final train departed nearly 30 minutes late from the crowded platform at Hayling Island across exploding detonators and into the moonlit night en route to Havant. Despite the coldness, people stood at the many vantage points along the line and the intermediate station platforms were full to overflowing. The return run in the cold crisp night alongside the backwaters of Langstone Harbour was a sight many would remember, and as the occupants of the crowded guard's van rendered 'Auld Lang Syne', the train finally eased round the curve over exploding detonators and into Havant at 9.50 pm. Here the station master was waiting to welcome the train's arrival in the glare of flashbulbs as many cameras recorded the occasion for posterity. With local people paying their last respects and singing 'Auld Lang Syne', London-bound passengers had to hurry over the footbridge to catch the last fast train to Waterloo, scheduled to depart at 9.34 pm, which had obligingly been held especially for travellers off the branch.

In contrast to the sadness of the previous day, the running of the last official passenger train on Sunday 3rd November brought a carnival atmosphere of a bank holiday. In bright sunlight the Locomotive Club of Great Britain's special 'Hayling Farewell' Railtour train conveyed over 450 enthusiasts for the last return run across the branch before official closure. The special was routed from Waterloo via Alton, Eastleigh and Portsmouth Dockyard. On arrival at Havant, the enthusiasts alighted from the main line stock and joined the five-coach branch special train, hauled by 'A1X' class 0-6-0 tank locomotives No. 32636 at the leading end, and No. 32670 at the trailing end of the stock. On the down run the train disgorged its passengers at Langston and North Hayling for photographic stops, and by the time the special train arrived at Hayling Island hundreds of local people and enthusiasts had turned out to see the 'Hayling Billy' for the last time. An overture of exploding detonators heralded the departure in brilliant sunshine of the last up train running non-stop to Havant. All along the route the cheers and waves of lineside spectators were acknowledged by whistles from the two locomotives and cheers and waves from passengers on the train. Even the hooting of a steam launch moored by the headquarters of Langstone Sailing Club added to the occasion. All too soon No. 32670 led the train round the curve into Havant station and with No. 32636 bringing up the rear, the Hayling Island branch was no more.

At the time of the branch closure a Southern Railway enamelled metal green sign at Langston, still proclaimed

LANGSTON TOLL BRIDGE
WARNING TO DRIVERS OF VEHICLES
BE PREPARED TO STOP
CLEAR OF THE GATE

After closure a group of enthusiasts created the Hayling Light Railway Society and formulated plans to reopen the line for passenger traffic, with ambitious proposals to use an electric tram service. Few local organizations or indeed individuals backed the idea and the scheme fell into oblivion. As a result of the failure, a sun saloon tram resurrected from Blackpool Corporation Tramways, No. 11 built in 1939 and withdrawn from service in October 1962, was bought for use on the line and stabled in the up side goods yard at Havant from 1965 until it was removed to the East Anglian Railway Museum, Carlton Colville, near Lowestoft in January 1969 for preservation.

Of greater significance was the early return of a 'Terrier' tank locomotive to the island. After withdrawal from traffic BR sold No. 32646 to the Hayling Terrier Fund for £750 but this venture was unsuccessful and it was sold on to the Sadler Railcar Co. and moved to Droxford on the Meon Valley line. Again the undertaking failed and the locomotive was purchased by Brickwoods brewery of Portsmouth. On 17th May, 1966 it was taken by low-loader to Hayling Island to stand outside the 'Hayling Billy' public house, where it was painted in Stroudley LBSCR livery with the original name *Newington* on the side tanks. In 1975 the Isle of Wight Steam Railway approached brewers Whitbread Wessex Ltd (who had taken over Brickwoods) to acquire the engine but it was 2nd June, 1979 before the decision was made (against competition) to let the locomotive return across the Solent. She arrived at Haven Street on 25th June, 1979 and has since served on the preserved line in her former island identity of No. 8 *Freshwater*.

Weeds gradually choked the railway trackbed as time passed but a short section of the single line at Havant was retained as a headshunt until it was taken out of use on 9th August, 1965 and New Lane level crossing gates were disconnected and secured across the railway. In 1966 British Rail contracted a Rickmansworth firm to remove the opening span of Langston bridge, and soon after the track was taken up. The entire branch from the Hayling side of New Lane level crossing was sold to Havant and Waterloo Urban District Council (which later became the Borough of Havant) on 29th March, 1967. By 1971 the intermediate stations had been demolished, although the buildings at Hayling Island were still in use but they were ultimately demolished, the canopy being dismantled and re-erected at the Hollycombe Steam Collection, a 2 ft gauge line operating near Liphook. Nothing now remains of Langston bridge except the piers on either side of the former opening span, which have been left to mark the channel for shipping, and railway bridge concrete bases. The area at Havant station used by the Hayling Island branch train was from late 1963 converted to a car park, whilst the bay platform was demolished in 1972. The remains of the *Carrier* jetty at Langston in the form of broken timber stumps appear at low tide to this day.

A 4½ mile coastal path for horse riders, cyclists and pedestrians follows the former route of the branch along the western extremity of the island and at its northernmost point just south of the remains of the railway bridge a signal post has been reconstructed as a reminder of the 'Hayling Billy'. The first section from New Lane, Havant to the Langstone Road was opened at a special ceremony held at 2.30 pm on Friday 30th August, 2002 at the site of New Lane gates. Councillor Gordon Erlebach, Mayor of the Borough of Havant and the Lady Mayoress attended. The Havant Borough Council Project Manager Martin Pettifer gave a short speech and the trail was opened by Stephen Norris MP, Chairman of the National Cycling Strategy Board, who cut a ribbon and then cycled down the newly shared path with David Willetts MP. A crowd of walkers, cyclists and mothers with pushchairs then followed along the 1.6 kilometre course, which had been provided as a joint venture by Hampshire County Council, Havant Borough Council, Sustrans and A.J. Bull Limited. A small reception was held after the event in the civic centre. The opening of the Hayling Billy Trail has thus provided easy access to Langstone Harbour, the former oyster bed workings and the local nature reserve created after the closure of the line with much to offer for lovers of flora, fauna and safe wind surfing. At the end of the line Hayling Island goods shed has been modernized and enlarged and serves as a theatre.

Chapter Five

The Route Described

Havant station, 78 miles 15 chains from Victoria via Dorking and 37 miles 24 chains from Brighton, was opened by the LBSCR on 15th March, 1847 and for 12 years remained unaltered until the LSWR reached the town with its 'direct Portsmouth' line on 1st January, 1859 forming a physical junction east of the station at 66 miles 18 chains from Waterloo and bringing it 66 miles 37 chains from London. The down side of the station was rebuilt in 1889 and the up side in 1894. The platforms were served by up and down main lines but as part of the Portsmouth electrification programme in 1937/1938 the station was completely rebuilt in pre-cast ferro-concrete in the SR 'Odeon' style with new platforms constructed to accommodate loop lines together with up and down through tracks enabling express services to pass slower traffic. The Hayling Island branch trains used the bay at the eastern end of the down platform served by a trailing connection from the up main line but with the 1937/38 station alterations a temporary platform was provided before the branch services were accommodated at the back of the new down bay platform. Connection to the branch was now made by a trailing connection from the down platform loop and a facing connection from the up loop, the branch traffic thus always remaining independent of the main lines. The bay platform, 430 ft in length could accommodate a maximum of five bogie coaches and a 'Terrier' tank locomotive, whilst by the buffer stops was a small water crane and coal stage used to replenish the branch engine. In addition to the platform line, branch facilities included the 480 ft-long run-round loop with 120 ft headshunt at the east end, and 340 ft-long Leggett's siding used for the stabling of additional coaching or wagon stock when not commercially required. Havant goods yard located to the north of the down main line platform was used for interchanging of traffic to and from the Hayling Island branch. The yard was closed on 6th January, 1969 and the track was lifted in May 1971.

On leaving the branch platform the Hayling Island single line branch swung sharply away to the south on an 8 chains radius right-hand curve passing over New Lane level crossing at 9 chains with gates worked initially by Havant Junction East signal box, renamed Havant Junction from 1918. When the 1937/38 alterations were made and Havant West ex-LBSCR signal box was abolished on 1st May, 1938 (Havant North ex-LSWR signal box had already been abolished on 3rd November, 1935 as a prelude to the work), Havant Junction was renamed plain Havant. The signal box was finally abolished on 29th October, 2007. The branch rising at 1 in 300 and then falling at 1 in 88/540 passed through a wide cutting on a 19 chains radius left-hand curve. East Street overbridge No. 1 carrying the A27 coast road over the line at 0 miles 25 ½ chains and wrought-iron footbridge No. 2 at 0 miles 32½ chains spanned the single line (Havant By-Pass overbridge No. 2A at 0 miles 48 chains was also planned), as the branch negotiated 27/62/22 chain right-hand curves on a 1 in 540 falling gradient. A straight course falling at 1 in 330 took the line through a shallow cutting and the residential area of Havant to the 1 mile post. On the outskirts of the town the branch continued on the falling gradient negotiating a 14 chains radius left-hand curve before crossing the main Havant to Hayling Island road to enter Langston station at 1 mile 09 chains from Havant on level track. After World War II and the increase in road transport, the level crossing was a constant

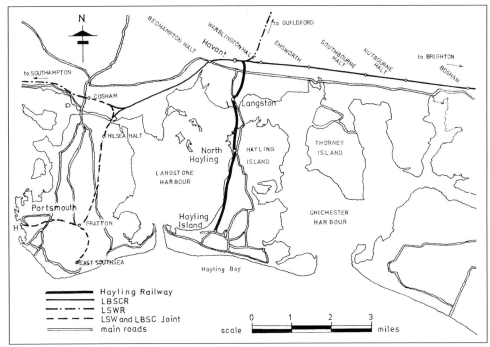

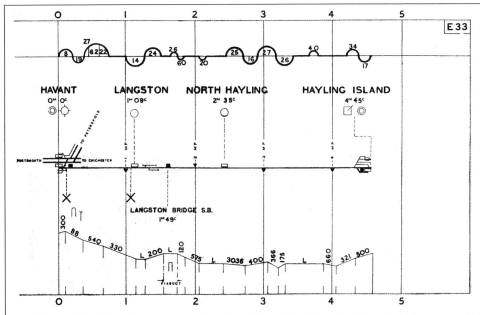

SR gradient and curvature diagram for the branch - some details differ from LBSCR figures.

Havant station facing towards Portsmouth with the Hayling Island branch train standing at the bay platform to the left. The ornate station buildings with the main offices are on the down platform, which like the up side is fronted by an ornate canopy. The platforms are connected by covered footbridge whilst in the background is Leigh Road level crossing guarded by Havant West signal box located on the up side of the line. *Author's Collection*

LBSCR Marsh-designed Atlantic 4-4-2 No. 37 stands in the up platform at Havant with a train for Brighton. The Hayling Island bay platform to the left is occupied by a set of Stroudley 4-wheel coaches, whilst the goods yard is to the right with end-on loading dock prominent. No. 37 was delivered in December 1905 to the LBSCR as class 'B5', later class 'H1', was named *Selsey Bill* by the SR and later renumbered 2037. *Author's Collection*

Havant LBSCR station building

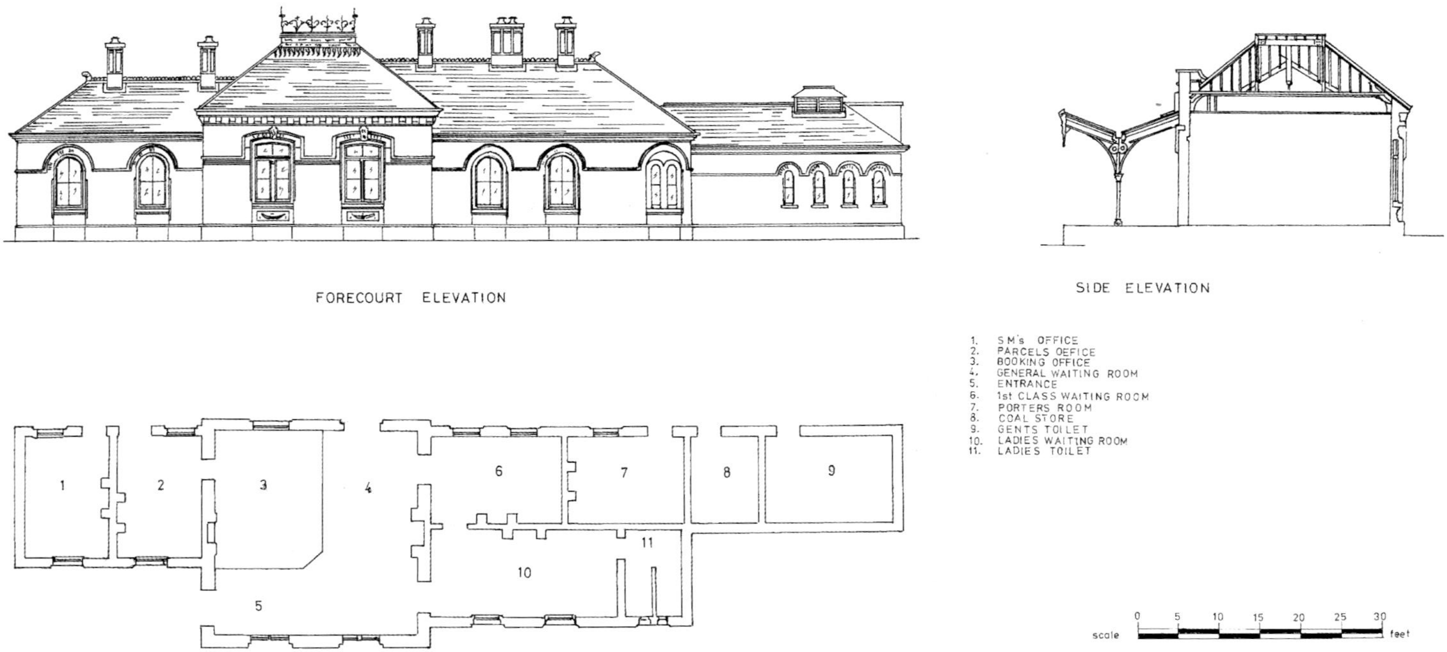

SIDE ELEVATION

FORECOURT ELEVATION

1. S.M's OFFICE
2. PARCELS OFFICE
3. BOOKING OFFICE
4. GENERAL WAITING ROOM
5. ENTRANCE
6. 1st CLASS WAITING ROOM
7. PORTERS ROOM
8. COAL STORE
9. GENTS TOILET
10. LADIES WAITING ROOM
11. LADIES TOILET

scale

0   5   10   15   20   25   30   feet

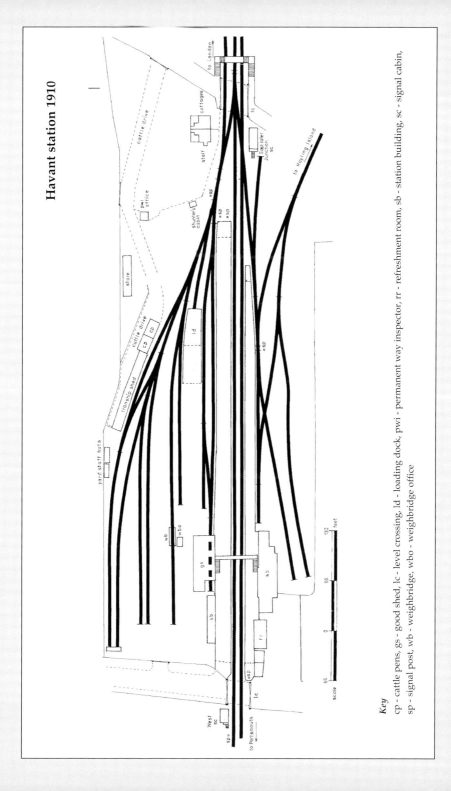

Havant station 1910

Key

cp - cattle pens, gs - good shed, lc - level crossing, ld - loading dock, pwi - permanent way inspector, rr - refreshment room, sb - station building, sc - signal cabin, sp - signal post, wb - weighbridge, wbo - weighbridge office

Havant station 1938

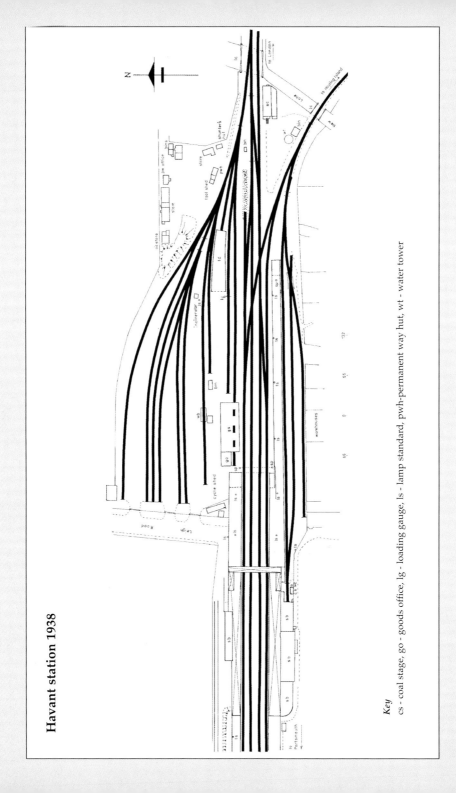

Key

cs - coal stage, go - goods office, lg - loading gauge, ls - lamp standard, pwh - permanent way hut, wt - water tower

A view of the bay platform and associated lines at Havant in 1962 with a 'Terrier' tank locomotive on the run-round loop and wagons stored in Leggett's siding. The down branch starting signal is upper quadrant on-rail post and behind that the station nameboard advises Havant for Hayling Island - hardly a necessary appendage when it faced the branch and passengers arriving and departing were well aware of the obvious!   *J. Scrace*

View facing east of the physical junction between the Hayling Island branch and the main line in 1930 before the electrification alterations. Havant signal box in the centre controls the double barrier gates on the Portsmouth to Brighton main line which itself is spanned by a footbridge for pedestrians. To the right is the Hayling Island branch curving away over New Lane level crossing with the combined up branch home and down branch advance starting signals on the same post beyond the gates. Ahead is the headshunt terminating just short of the signal box whilst the grounded coach body behind the water tank provided staff accommodation.

Author's Collection

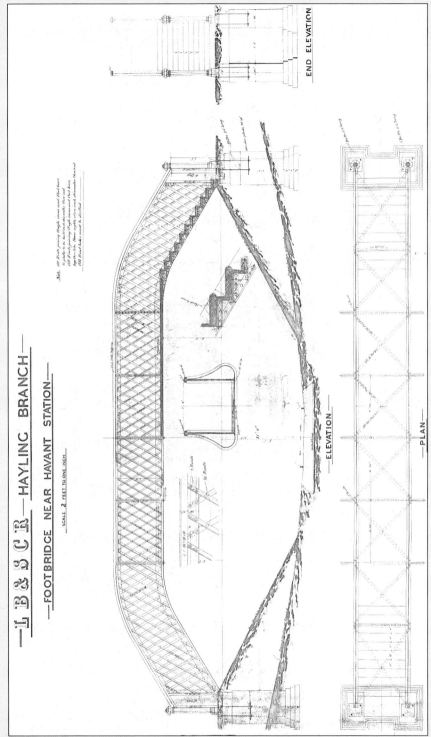

LBSCR drawing of footbridge No. 2 at 00 miles 32½ chains between Havant and Langston.

inconvenience to motorists, especially on summer Saturdays when the half-hourly train service in each direction brought traffic to a standstill, often with the queue trailing for anything up to two miles back along the road. The gates were hand operated and together with the associated signalling were released by a 6-lever ground frame, latterly an ex-LSWR McKenzie & Holland frame situated on the up side of the line close to the crossing. Usually one man operated the ground frame and gates, but at busy periods two men worked the crossing to minimize the inconvenience. Just before closure of the line one of the level crossing gates was severely damaged by a car and was removed.

Langston station initially had a single timber platform 150 ft in length on the down side of the line, adjoining the main road. The original timber platform was replaced during SR days and then in 1949/50 by a 200 ft-long pre-stressed concrete platform, which was originally destined for use at North Hayling but not used. A simple waiting shelter, in two sections dating from separate periods and complete with small canopy, was provided at the south end of the platform but in 1897 this decrepit structure was replaced by a new timber building located nearer the level crossing gates and adorned with the usual advertisement hoardings. This building contained a booking office and waiting room, which doubled up as a ladder store. The separate waiting room section was abolished in 1908 and waiting facilities were provided in the booking hall. Two oil lamps, nameboard, platform seat and backing fence completed the facilities.

Beyond the halt the line continued on the level passing Langston Bridge down distant and Langston Crossing up home signals sharing the same post on the up side of the line before climbing at 1 in 200 on a 24 chains radius right-hand curve passing the short engineer's siding with facing points for down traffic on the down side of the single line where catch points were located 75 yards from the connection with the running line. Access to this siding was obtained from a ground frame released by a key attached to the single line Train Staff, and it was usual in the latter years for wagons to be propelled from Havant. The keys to the gate protecting this siding were obtained from the staff at Langston. In the heyday of the line two sets of sidings were provided to serve Langston Quay, the down side sidings, 980 ft in length with a 320 ft headshunt at the north end, served coal wharves, which ceased to be used in the 1890s after which they were used by the engineer's department. The siding on the up side with points controlled from a ground frame was on a 1 in 200 falling gradient towards Langston and was equipped with catch points located 46 yards from the connection with the main line. The facility was 790 ft in length complete with a short run-round loop (later removed) and served a merchandise wharf. Originally this siding was installed for the transference of wagons to the Isle of Wight by the *Carrier* train ferry. Soon after the SR assumed responsibilities for the line both up and down side sidings were considerably shortened. During World War II heavy armaments arriving by road were restricted from crossing Langstone road bridge because of severe weight restrictions and the plan was to dismantle the equipment and transfer to railway wagons for conveyance on to Hayling Island. To facilitate the transfer an extra siding with an end loading dock was provided on the down side but unfortunately not until 1951, six years after the cessation of hostilities! The up side sidings were removed in 1944 whilst that on the down side except for a short section used by the engineer's department were finally removed as the wharves had long since fallen into disuse.

The main single branch line continued on a long right-hand 24 chains radius curve climbing at 1 in 200 towards Langston bridge where a 20 mph speed limit was

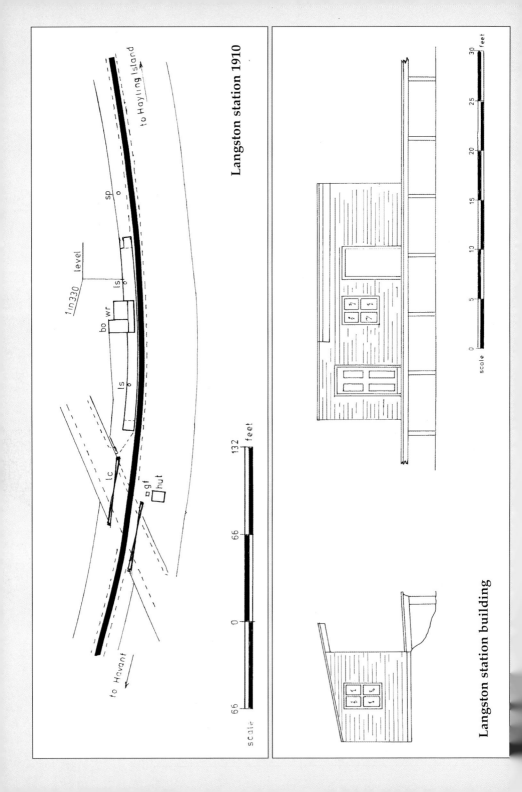

Langston station 1910

Langston station building

A view of the early Langston station with short platform and combined booking office and waiting room facing towards Havant with the slotted up starting signal protecting the level crossing gates. Note the spectacle lamp is mounted lower down the signal post than the arm. The crossing keeper/porter-in-charge's cottage stands on the opposite side of the road from the station in, at the time, a rural location. *Author's Collection*

The run-down and decrepit apology for a station at Langston with a down train approaching. The short timber platform appears to be subsiding while the surface is very uneven. The timber station building including booking office and waiting room certainly requires refurbishment, whilst the two platform oil lamps appear to be the most modern accoutrements on show. In the background is the original cottage provided for the accommodation of the local crossing keeeper/porter-in-charge. *Author's Collection*

Langston station 1 mile 09 chains from Havant viewed facing north and showing the level crossing gates on 29th October, 1962.   *Ken Paye*

Close-up view of the timber station building at Langston, view facing towards Havant. Electric lighting has replaced the former oil lamps.   *Author's Collection*

The up afternoon mixed train from Hayling Island to Havant entering Langston behind No. 32650 on 29th October, 1962. Mixed train working continued on the branch long after similar services had been withdrawn elsewhere on BR. The amount of goods traffic on the branch did not warrant the running of a separate freight train in each direction and the frequency of the passenger service precluded a path being available. *Ken Paye*

The down side sidings at Langston viewed from a passing train in 1960. Although the commercial gravel, timber and coal traffic ceased in the 1890, the siding was retained for use of the civil engineers in connection with track maintenance and remedial repairs to the swing bridge. The points at the entrance to the siding were controlled by a ground frame released by Annett's key on the single line Train Staff. *A.E. Bennett*

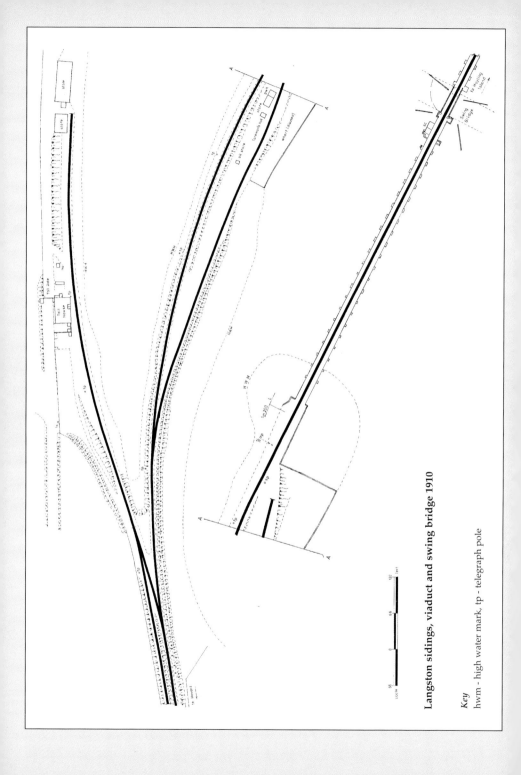

Langston sidings, viaduct and swing bridge 1910

Key
hwm - high water mark, tp - telegraph pole

With the swing span at its fullest open position a vessel passes Langston bridge. The red flag displayed indicated to captains of vessels that they had to tie up at the adjacent mooring posts prior to passing or warping through the gap, that the bridge was fully open and ready. When this procedure was in operation no trains were permitted to depart from Havant or Hayling Island towards the bridge. *Author's Collection*

The centre opening portion of Langston swing bridge view facing towards Havant with Langston Bridge signal box to the right. At the far end of the timber structure on the up side of the line is the post carrying Langston Bridge up starting signal, lower arm and down home signal, upper arm mounted on the same post. Langston Bridge signal box, a non-block post, was of timber construction measuring 9 ft 9 in. by 8 ft 9 in. with operating floor 4 ft 6 in. above rail level and contained a 7-lever frame. *Author's Collection*

Langston bridge from the north with No. 32650 approaching the timber structure with a down train on 29th October, 1962. Langston Bridge signal box can be seen on the down side of the line whilst the signal post to the right supports Langston Bridge down home signal and Langston station up distant whose arm is just visible.

Ken Paye

Langston Bridge from the south end in November 1962 showing that the structure curved at 26 chains radius before the line reached terra firma on Hayling Island.

Author

The opening span of Langston swing bridge viewed from Langston Bridge signal box showing the locking mechanism and the signal wires which had to be disconnected when the span was open for shipping.   *Ken Paye*

The close proximity of the waters of Langstone Harbour to the Hayling Island branch is evident in this view of an up train hauled by No. 32650 approaching the south end of Langston bridge on 29th October, 1962. Because of constant tidal erosion it was necessary to provide hardcore and concrete protection to prevent the waters undermining the trackbed during periods of exceptionally high tides.   *Ken Paye*

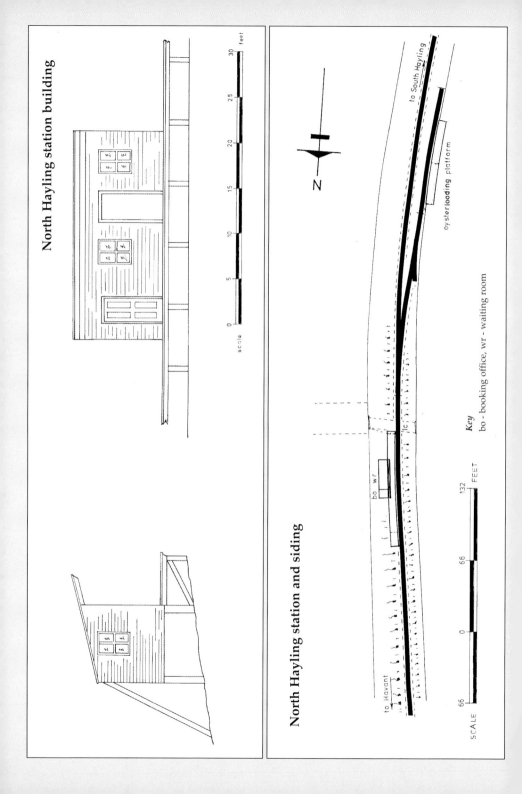

North Hayling station building

scale

0　5　10　15　20　25　30　feet

North Hayling station and siding

N

to South Hayling

oyster loading platform

bo　wr

to Havant

Key
bo - booking office, wr - waiting room

SCALE

66　0　66　132　FEET

enforced across the structure. Langston bridge, 1 mile 49 chains from Havant, crossed on level track, was of the timber trestle type and carried the railway across the waterway separating Hayling Island from the mainland. Some 1,100 ft in length with a high iron-retaining rail on each side of the track at rail level and a 50 ft opening centre span, the bridge carried the branch 23 feet above the deepest cut in the navigable channel. To control the opening and closing of the span a small timber signal box, Langston Bridge box, was perched alongside the bridge on the down side of the line north of the opening span. The signal box was regularly manned until 1938 and then only staffed when the span required opening. The box closed on 17th September, 1963 when the associated signal arms were removed but not abolished until 4th November, 1963. The timber viaduct, carried on 50 trestles, from 1926 to 1931 bedded in concrete, was located parallel to and an eighth of a mile west of the modern concrete road bridge, which was opened on 10th September, 1956, five months ahead of schedule, to replace the cramped and inconvenient single lane wooden toll bridge. As with Langston level crossing, the old road bridge had been a constant source of complaints by motorists, but railway staff continued to collect tolls, on behalf of Hampshire County Council until 11th April, 1960.

Leaving the bridge on a 26 chains right-hand curve the branch then fell at 1 in 120 round a short 60 chains left-hand curve before following a straight course descending at 1 in 575 past the site of the abandoned Oyster Creek oyster beds and the 2 mile post. From here eight chains of the abandoned railway embankment of the original formation could be seen on the up side of the line, with a longer stretch near Sinah Point. The branch continued its straight and level course along the west coast of Hayling Island interspersed by a short 20 chains left-hand curve. Never far from the tidal waters of Langstone Harbour, the line soon entered North Hayling, 2 miles 35 chains from Havant.

The station referred to as a halt, but not officially titled as such, located on the down side of the line consisted of a raised timber platform 150 ft in length and a timber building similar to that at Langston complete with booking office, booking hall and waiting room. These facilities proved excessive for the remote location but ticket issuing remained as the member of staff was also employed to operate points to the siding beyond the halt. When this facility closed in 1907 the member of station staff was withdrawn and a simple wooden shelter replaced the original building with the nameboard placed above the opening for passengers. A wooden fence at the back of the platform and a solitary post for an oil or tilley lamp completed the amenities. The halt was exposed to the elements and a gravel track, which continued across the railway south of the platform, connected the station with the backwaters and the main road. In 1908 only two houses stood in Station Road; in later years considerable housing development was made in the area but away from the railway. After closure or the booking office the guard thereafter issued tickets to passengers from a hand-held ticket rack. A new enamel sign denoting 'North Hayling Halt' was made in 1949 but was never erected, remaining in store at Havant until after the line closed. On several occasions, visitors to the shoreline having been stranded by the rising tide had to be rescued by emergency services alerted by passengers waiting on the platform or passing in the train.

Shortly after leaving the platform at North Hayling facing points in the main single line led to a short siding on the up side of the railway serving an oyster loading stage and ramp, which was shunted by trains travelling in the up direction. The siding was originally planned to be located with points slightly to the north of the platform with the loading stage and ramp to the west of the siding but the ground was found unstable and the connection and siding was relocated to more substantial terrain. From 1907,

North Hayling station facing towards Havant *circa* 1900. The building on the platform contained a booking office and waiting room and the station was staffed until 1907. Note the large station nameboard, steps instead of a ramp at the end of the platform and a collection of milk churns on the platform.   *Roger Nash Collection*

The simple all-timber North Hayling station 2 miles 35 chains from Havant with platform 150 ft in length viewed facing north in November 1962 with North Hayling crossing No. 8 in foreground.   *Author*

North Hayling station from the foreshore of Langstone Harbour on 17th July, 1958.

H.C. Casserley

North Hayling station on the edge of Langstone Harbour served the remote north-western area of Hayling Island and compared with other stations on the branch relatively few passengers used the facilities. Of all timber construction the station at least possessed a waiting room for intending passengers to shelter from the prevailing south-west winds and inclement weather. 'Terrier' 0-6-0T No. 32650 pulls into the platform with a down train on 29th October, 1962.

Ken Paye

View facing north towards Havant from the platform at Hayling Island on 3rd September, 1952. To the left is the bay platform road protected by an LBSCR starting signal, whilst the main platform road has the SR starter in the 'clear' position. Other lines fanning out from the station throat from left to right are the run-round loop, dock road and shed road. The signal box is at the end of the platform and the signalmen's lobby containing the block instruments is beside the bay platform road.   *H.C. Casserley*

Hayling Island station facing towards the buffer stops in the 1930s. A 'Terrier' 0-6-0T locomotive waits in the main platform with her train for Havant. The LBSCR-style station nameboard is prominent on the platform whilst to the left of the run-round loop is the locomotive coaling stage. The rural location of the branch terminus in enhanced by two haystacks in the adjacent field.   *Author's Collection*

after the withdrawal of the station staff, the guard operated the points to the siding which was out of use by 1925 and was removed soon after. Beyond the siding the branch swung on a 25 chains right-hand curve falling at 1 in 3036 past farmland which later gave way to market gardens. On the up side of the line the waters of Langstone Harbour lapped close to the foundations of the track as the railway curved to the left on a 16 chains radius curve rising at 1 in 400 followed by a 27 chains right-hand curve past the 3 mile post, Knott's Marsh and abandoned oyster beds. The 1 in 400 rise continued for a short distance to a minor summit before the line descended at 1 in 366 and then climbed at 1 in 175 whilst negotiating a 26 chains left-hand curve. A straight section on the level followed by a 40 chains radius right-hand curve kept the line close to the western shore of the island. A further level and straight section was followed by 1 in 660 falling to the 4 mile post, with distant views of Southsea to the south-west. The backwaters were left behind as the railway swung inland rising at 1 in 321 past Hayling Island fixed distant signal and around a 34 chain right-hand and 17 chains left-hand curve past the splitting home signals to enter Hayling Island terminus, 4 miles 45 chains from Havant on a 1 in 500 rising gradient, with the buffer stops at 4 miles 50 chains.

Situated away from the main centre of population of this scattered community at West Town, about half a mile from the south coast, the station had a main platform 420 feet in length and a bay platform 330 ft long, the latter used except on summer Saturdays for the storage of spare coaching stock. The brick-built station originally called Hayling Island, then South Hayling from August 1869 until reverting to Hayling Island from 1st June, 1892 was constructed in the Gothic style by F. Whitaker, incorporating timber framing with inset red and white herringbone brickwork dated from the opening of the line, and the large canopy fronting the building and over the platform was added at a later date. This canopy in front of the station building received damage from a bomb blast in World War II and was dismantled and never replaced. The track layout consisted of the main platform line, which terminated at buffer stops beside the station approach. The 780 ft-long run-round loop parallel to the platform line enabled the engine to run-round the train and next to that was 540 ft-long middle or dock siding for storage of coaching stock.

A general view of the track layout at Hayling Island facing south in 1962 with from left, back or coal road, shed road serving the commodious goods shed, dock road run-round loop, with coal stage alongside, main platform road and bay platform road with an up train for Havant waiting to depart.   *J. Scrace*

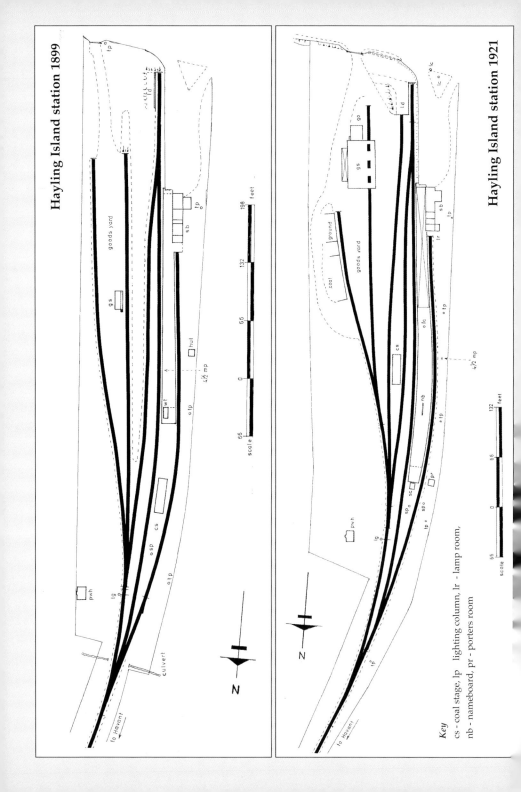

Hayling Island station 1899

Hayling Island station 1921

Key
cs - coal stage, lp lighting column, lr - lamp room,
nb - nameboard, pr - porters room

Hayling Island station facing towards the buffer stops in the 1930s, with the bay platform to the right, main single platform line to the left and alongside that the run-round loop. Open wagons are berthed on the dock road and the commodious goods shed is to the left. *Author's Collection*

Hayling Island station from the north facing the buffer stops with, from left to right, covered vans occupying the dock road, 'Terrier' tank locomotive by the coal stage on the run-round loop, a three-coach train with BR standard non-gangway stock in the main platform and to the right the bay platform road. The miniscule signal box containing 10 levers is at the end of the platform behind the rail-mounted up starting signal, whilst giving protection to the bay platform road is the former LBSCR lower quadrant starting signal. The building to the right is the staff lobby which contained block instruments. *Author's Collection*

A close-up view of the full canopy at Hayling Island station in the early 1900s, with a 'Terrier' 0-6-0T locomotive arriving with a branch train. Viewed from the goods yard, it shows two six-wheel vehicles stabled by the buffer stops in the bay platform road.   *Author's Collection*

A close-up view of the ornate station buildings provided at Hayling Island, fully exposed after the removal of the south end of the canopy because of structural deterioration and bomb blast damage. In this late 1950s view a covered van is stabled with Maunsell stock in the bay platform to the right.   *Author's Collection*

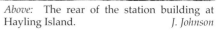

Above: The rear of the station building at Hayling Island. *J. Johnson*

Left: Detail of the ornate brickwork and tiling provided on Hayling Island station booking office extension dating from 1896. *J. Johnson*

Hayling Island goods shed

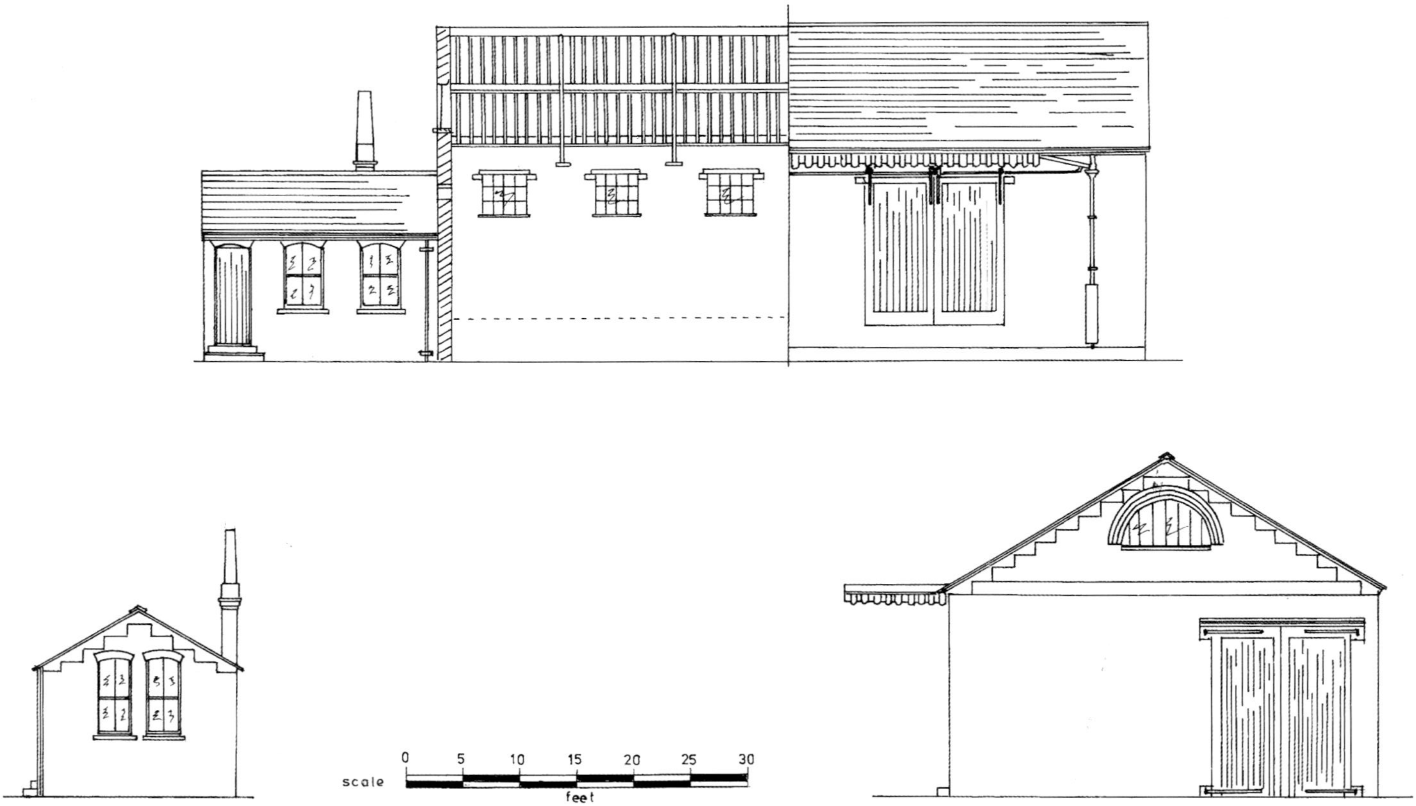

scale

0 5 10 15 20 25 30
feet

Western aspect of the goods shed at Hayling Island provided in 1900. Building materials, agricultural machinery and products and 'smalls' traffic for local shops were handled sometimes using the 1½ ton capacity crane located on the loading bank of the structure. In the last five years the shed saw little use as freight traffic dwindled and a road crane was then employed for any lifting requirement. *J. Johnson*

The north end of the goods shed at Hayling Island showing the sliding doors fitted in the latter years. *J. Johnson*

'Terrier' 0-6-0T No. 32650 runs round her train at Hayling Island on 29th October, 1963, shadowed by the wall of the goods shed. *R. Powell*

Across the goods yard roadway were two sidings, the 420 ft shed road which served the commodious 63 ft by 38 ft goods shed standing by the main gate to the yard and the 290 ft back or coal road serving coal grounds. Adjacent to the run-round loop was a coal stage for the replenishment of the branch locomotive. A 1 ton 10 cwt capacity fixed crane stood in the goods shed but latterly any lifting required was carried out by a mobile road crane. At the north end of the platform separate starting signals were located for the main and bay line departures. Points and signals at Hayling Island were controlled from a small 10-lever ground level signal box situated at the north end of the platform. It was possible for an engine to run-round 35 trucks at the terminus, although the load limit on the branch was 25 vehicles.

The speed limit on the branch in the early years was 20 mph but as the track improved a speed limit of 35 mph was imposed with 20 mph over Langston bridge. Standard Southern Railway concrete mileposts were located on the up side of the line whilst a mixture of wooden and concrete gradient posts were sited on the down side of the track.

Hayling Island station facing towards the buffers stops with the goods shed to the left and the entrance gate to the goods yard. The covered van is standing on dock road beside the end-on loading dock, whilst the run-round loop and main single platform line converge on the buffers stops. Note the plethora of barrows at the end of the platform. *Author's Collection*

Chapter Six

Permanent Way, Signalling and Staff

Permanent Way

The original permanent way of the Hayling Railway was formed of bridge pattern rails for the first 3 miles 64 chains from Havant. Weighing 80 lbs per yard and in lengths of 24 ft, they were laid on sleepers placed 2 ft 3 in. apart. The remainder of the line was laid with flat bottom rails weighing 70 lb. per yard, again in 24 ft lengths. The rails were fastened to the sleepers at the fishplated joints by fang bolts, as were the centre of the rails, whilst coach screws were utilized at the other intermediate sleepers. The sleepers were 9 ft x 10 in. x 4½ in., rectangular at the joints and half-round in shape elsewhere. The ballast consisted of either gravel or shingle or a mixture of both, laid to a depth of one foot below the sleepers. In 1889 the bridge pattern rails were replaced by 58 lb. per yard flat bottom track but 10 years later the entire line was re-laid using 78 lb. per yard bullhead rails, except on Langston bridge where flat bottom track was retained. In later years the SR used bullhead track of 87 and 90 lb. per yard plus some second-hand material removed from the main line, whilst British Standard rails of 90 and 95 lb. per yard were introduced after nationalization. In 1952 part of the line between Havant and Langston was laid with concrete sleepers. Throughout the life of the line one gang based at Havant maintained the permanent way. In the latter years permanent way staff based at Havant for the Hayling Island branch included Ron Sitwell, David Lear and Jock Wright.

Signalling

From the outset the single line was worked on the Train Staff and Ticket principle with Train Staff stations at Havant and South Hayling, later Hayling Island. There were no crossing places and if two trains used the line travelling in the same direction, the driver of the first train carried a Ticket after being shown the Train Staff, whilst the driver of the second train conveyed the Train Staff. By 1892 the LBSCR had standardized the Electric Train Staff for single line working with few exceptions, one of which was Havant to Hayling Island, which retained Train Staff and Ticket. Langston Bridge signal box was a Train Staff and Ticket block post non-crossing station where a closing switch was provided. The box was only used when the swing bridge required opening and closing. The Train Staff had a handle at one end and was lettered in blue 'Havant and Hayling Island', the colour of the paper Train Staff Tickets and the Ticket Box were also blue. Later the handle on the Train Staff was in the centre. The key on the Train Staff controlled entry to Langston sidings 330 yds and 435 yds south of Langston station respectively as well as the siding at North Hayling. At Havant the person authorized to receive and deliver the Train Staff or Train Staff Ticket was the station master or a porter specially deputed by the station master whilst at Hayling Island the signalman or porter-signalman was responsible. From about 1890 the single line Train Staff method of operation was used in conjunction with block signalling with Havant Junction, Langston Bridge and South Hayling, later Hayling Island signal boxes being equipped with Tyer's one-wire two position block instruments.

99

Permanent way work is in progress on Langston bridge as a 'Terrier' 0-6-0T approaches with a down train from Havant. To the left can be seen the remains of loading ramp and cradle used by the unsuccessful *Carrier* train ferry service to St Helens, Isle of Wight. In the early years the locomotive working the branch often worked bunker first to South Hayling/ Hayling Island whereas in the latter years the engine invariably worked boiler first to Hayling Island.

Author's Collection

With the up starting signal cleared, No. 32650 drifts on to the coaching stock at Hayling Island prior to departing for Havant on 29th October, 1962. The small signal box measuring 6 ft by 6 ft containing a 10-lever LBSCR Tappet frame with 5 in. centres is to the left. *Ken Paye*

In the early years a small ground frame signal box was located at Havant, but as the LBSCR made improvements Havant Junction East signal box, of timber construction was opened in December 1858 and equipped with a Saxby frame. This was abolished on 25th June, 1876 and replaced by a brick structure measuring 30 ft x 12 ft with the operating floor 9 ft 9 in. above rail level and equipped with a 52-lever Saxby & Farmer frame with 5 in. centres. This box was extended in 1938 and equipped with an 80-lever Westinghouse 'A2' frame with 4 in. centres, operational from 1st May. The signal box was abolished on 29th October, 2007 when signalling came under the control of the Havant Area signalling centre using the same building. Over the years the signal box at the junction was retitled: Havant Junction East being replaced by Havant Junction in 1918 and then Havant with effect from 1st May, 1938, the latter with the signal prefix code 'KW'. At the west end of Havant station Havant West signal box was also opened on 25th June, 1876; of brick construction and measuring 18 ft x 12 ft with operating floor 5 ft 8 in. above rail level it was equipped with a 20-lever Saxby & Farmer frame with 5 in. centres and was abolished on 1st May, 1938

At Langston a small ground frame located by a hut measuring 6 ft x 6 ft was situated on the up side of the line. The 6-lever ground frame controlled the gate lock and released the home and distant signals. The original frame was replaced in later years by a McKenzie & Holland 6-lever tappet frame dating from 1911 originally supplied to the LSWR. The level crossing gates were hand worked by the crossing keeper after being released from the ground frame. The crossing keeper at Langston was advised of train movements by a repeater bell, which sounded when trains were block signalled by Havant signalman to Hayling Island and by the Hayling Island signalman to Havant. The repeat bell signal was also sounded when any signalling was made to or from Langston Bridge signal box (i.e. if it was in use).

Langston Bridge signal box perched alongside the bridge to the north of the opening span on the down or east side of the line was a block post non-crossing station opened in 1884. Of timber construction the structure measured 9 ft 9 in. x 8 ft 9 in. with operating floor 4 ft 6 in. above rail level. It was equipped with a 7-lever LBSCR Tappet frame with 5 in. centres with six working and one spare lever and contained the necessary mechanism to control the swing bridge. Railway protection was afforded by distant and home signals in each direction of travel, although the signal lamps were not lit unless the bridge was manned after Grouping. The signal box was closed 17th September, 1963 but not abolished until 4th November, 1963.

At Hayling Island a small ground level signal box was located at the north end of the platform between the main and bay platform lines and in 1902 was replaced by a new timber structure measuring 6 ft x 6 ft containing an LBSCR 10-lever tappet frame with 5 in. centres which controlled the points and signals at the terminus and its adjacent goods yard. Because of the lack of space the Tyer's block instruments were contained in the adjacent signalmen's lobby. For many years LBSCR lower quadrant signals were standard on the branch but over the final decade these were replaced by SR upper quadrant signals except for the bay platform starter at Hayling Island, which was still LBSCR lower quadrant when the line closed. This signal was removed to Clapham Museum after the line closed. Because of the nature of the service during fog and falling snow fogsignalmen were not provided at the following signals: Havant Junction from Hayling Island branch distant, Langston level crossing up and down distants, Langston Bridge up and down distants and Hayling Island down distant. In the event of deterioration of the weather staff at each station on the branch were to keep their colleagues informed by telegraph or telephone of conditions.

Right: The down home bracket signal on the approach to Hayling Island station, with LBSCR wooden lower quadrant arms and wooden post. The left-hand arm in the clear position designates the route to the main platform whilst the right-hand arm is for the bay platform road.
Author's Collection

Below: The rear view of Hayling Island's bracketed home signal. Standard SR upper quadrant arms on rail posts, replaced the signal in the latter years.
Author's Collection

Below right: Hayling Island up advance starting signal with LBSCR wooden lower quadrant arm on the up or west side of the single line just beyond the station throat. The signal was later replaced by an upper quadrant arm on rail posts.   *A.E. West*

Left: LBSCR lower quadrant up starting signal at Hayling Island, which controlled departures from the bay platform. The signal survived until closure of the line in November 1963. *Author*

Below left: The up and down distant signals sharing the same post just north of Langston, the left-hand or upper arm is Langston crossing fixed distant and the right-hand arm Havant up fixed distant.
Author's Collection

Below: The bracketed up branch home signal mounted on rail post on the approach to Havant, the left-hand arm authorizing entry to the Hayling Island bay platform and the right arm access to the down main platform line. Note the KW 69 on the plaque below the colour light signal denoted the lever number in Havant signal box. The signal in the background is Havant's branch advance starter.
Author's Collection

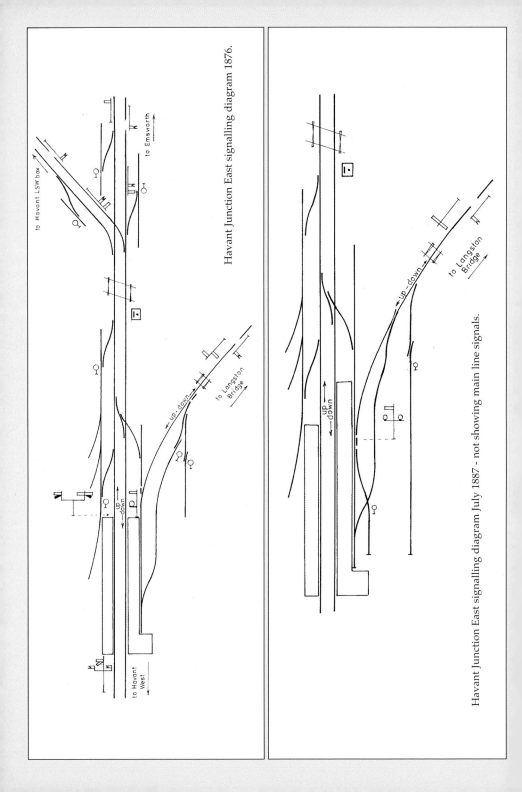

Havant Junction East signalling diagram 1876.

Havant Junction East signalling diagram July 1887 - not showing main line signals.

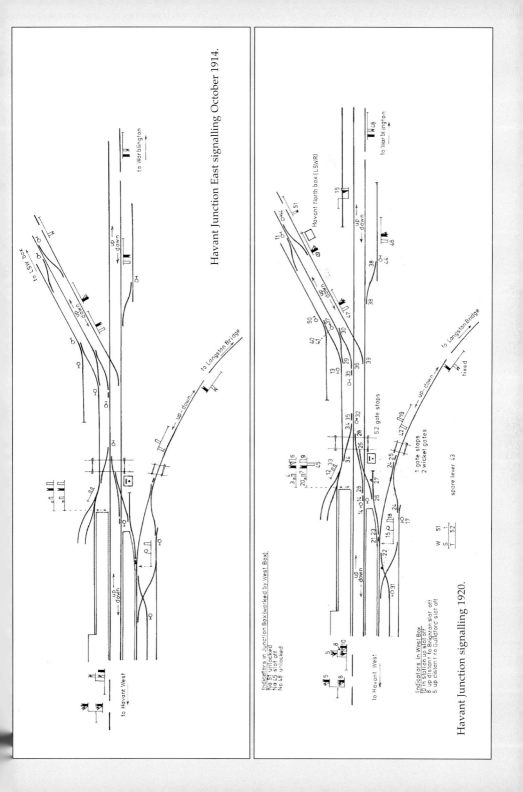

Havant Junction East signalling October 1914.

to Warblington

up
down

to LSW box

up
down

to Langston Bridge

up — down —

Havant Junction signalling 1920.

Havant North box (LSWR)

to Warblington

up
down

to Langston Bridge

fixed

up — down

1 gate stops
2 wickel gates

52 gate stops

spare lever 43

to Havant West

up
down

Indicators in Junction Box (worked by West Box)
No 51 unlocked
No 45 slot off
No 48 unlocked

Indicators in West Box
10 in station up slot off
8 up distant to Brighton slot off
5 up distant to Guildford slot off

W 51
S   1
T 52

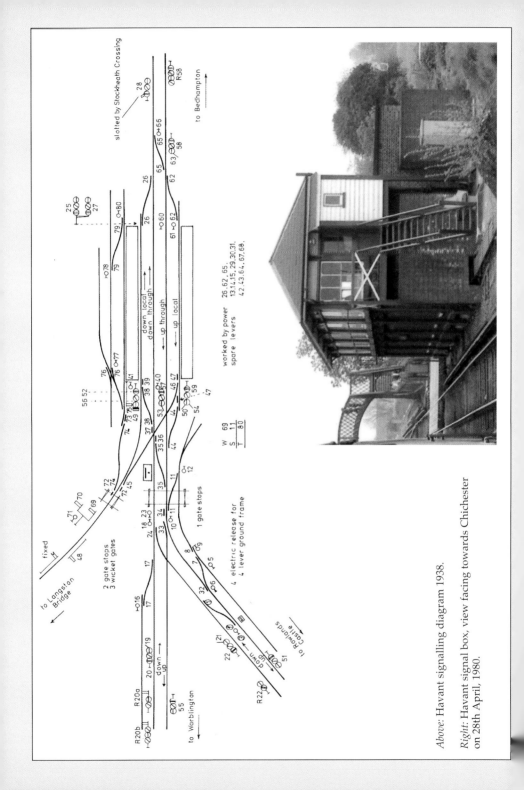

Above: Havant signalling diagram 1938.

Right: Havant signal box, view facing towards Chichester on 28th April, 1980.

In later LBSCR years Havant Junction East, from 1918 Havant Junction, signal box located on the down side of the main line at the east end of the station close to the crossing gates was open from 5.00 am on Mondays until 12.00 midnight the following Sunday as was Havant West signal box 787 yards to the west on the up side of the line at the west end of the station, close to level crossing gates. With the electrification work at Havant in 1937/38 Havant North ex-LSWR signal box (closed 3rd November, 1935) and Havant West signal box (closed 1st May, 1938) were abolished, and Havant Junction was renamed Havant from 1st May, 1938. The signal box was abolished on 29th October, 2007. On the branch Langston Level Crossing ground frame, 1,752 yards from Havant Junction signal box, which was not a block post, was open before the passage of the first booked train and closed after the passing of the last train. Langston Bridge signal box, a further 920 yds distant on the down side of the swing bridge north of the opening section, was open from 7.30 am until 3.30 pm or from 9.30 am until 5.30 pm or according to the tide. At other times the signal box was switched out and signal arms lowered, although the signal lights were left burning. Hayling Island Station signal box 2 miles 1,496 yards (LBSCR) or 2 miles 1,492 yards (SR) from Langston Bridge signal box and located on the up side at the north end of the station platform was open on weekdays from 6.45 am until 8.45 pm during winter months and 10.45 pm during the summer on weekdays and 9.45 am until 8.45 pm on Sundays during the summer. By 1962 Havant signal box was open continuously, Langston Bridge signal box 1 mile 912 yards from Havant signal box, was only open as required whilst Hayling Island signal box was open from 6.15 am until 9.15 pm on weekdays and 10.15 am until 8.15 pm on summer Sundays. When closed the signals were left at danger but the signal lights were left burning. The signal box was closed on Sundays during the winter. The entire branch was also closed on weekdays and Sundays after the passing of the last train until the running of the first train the next morning.

Navigational rights were extended round Hayling Island throughout the existence of the railway and for this reason Langston bridge had an opening span, which was controlled by the adjacent Langston Bridge signal box. The box controlled home and distant signals for each direction of travel, suitably interlocked with the lever working the bolt, which secured the bridge in position for the passage of trains, so that the bridge could not be opened unless all signals were at danger. When the bridge span required to be opened for shipping, the signalman at Langston Bridge signal box placed or maintained his signals at danger provided 'line clear' had not been given for a train or engine to approach from either Havant or Hayling Island and gave the 'opening bridge' bell signal 6-pause-6 to Hayling Island and Havant signalmen and received an acknowledgement of the signal from each place. He was also required to maintain the block signalling instrument in the 'line blocked' position. Having satisfied himself that no train or engine was approaching from either direction the bridge could be opened for the passage of a vessel or vessels to or from Langstone Harbour. In case of fog, platelayers were to be employed to place detonators on the rails at Langston Bridge distant signals in each direction. The signalmen at Havant and Hayling Island having received the 'opening bridge' signal were to acknowledge the call and place or maintain all signals for the line towards Langston to danger and keep them so until the 'obstruction removed' signal 7-pause-3-pause-4 was received after which normal working could be resumed. The opening of the bridge span necessitating the services of both a signalman and platelayer, the signalman being responsible for disconnecting the signal wires crossing the span, whilst the platelayer (later lengthman) unbolted the fishplates connecting the rails on the fixed and

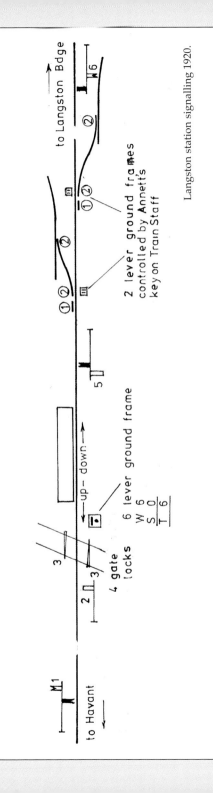

Langston station signalling 1920.

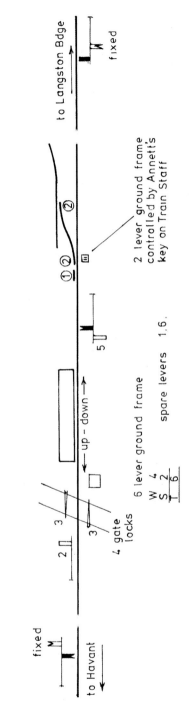

Langston station signalling 1931.

Trains departing in the up direction from Langston immediately crossed the main Havant to Hayling Island road by level crossing No. 4 where double gates were provided. Here the driver of No. 32640 leans out of his cab to watch for the guard's 'right way' on 20th July, 1949. The small cabin provided for the crossing keeper and his assistant is to the right whilst the 6-lever ground frame is alongside. *A.E. Wright*

Langston station facing towards Hayling Island with timber platform and timber station building located on the 14 chains radius curve. In the foreground is the 6-lever ground frame controlling the level crossing locking and associated signalling. *Author's Collection*

Langston Bridge signalling 1910.

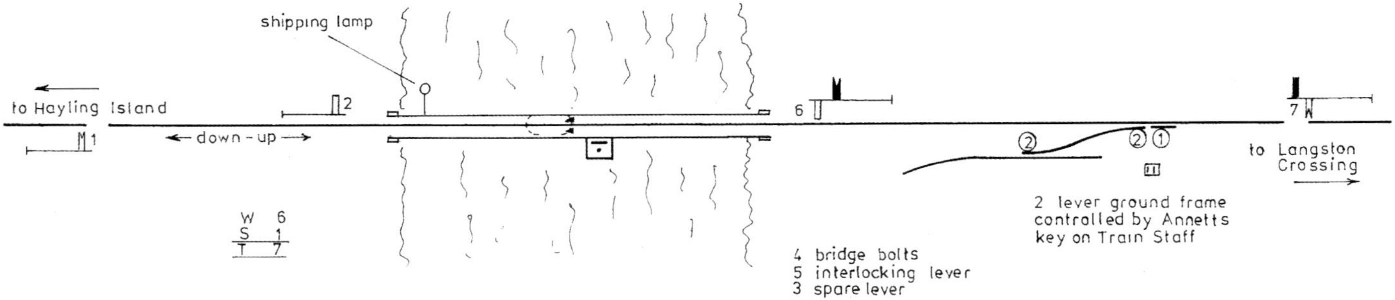
shipping lamp
to Hayling Island
1
2
down - up
6
7
to Langston Crossing
2
2
1
W 6
S 1
T 7
4 bridge bolts
5 interlocking lever
3 spare lever
2 lever ground frame controlled by Annetts key on Train Staff

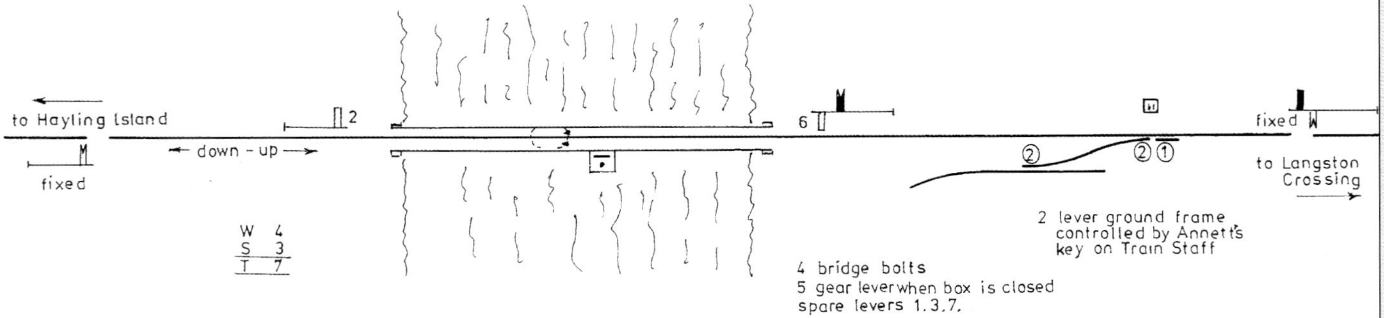
to Hayling Island
fixed
2
down - up
6
fixed
to Langston Crossing
2
2
1
W 4
S 3
T 7
4 bridge bolts
5 gear lever when box is closed
spare levers 1.3.7.
2 lever ground frame controlled by Annett's key on Train Staff

Langston Bridge signalling October 1951.

moveable sections of the bridge. Both men were required to open and close the bridge and after it had been used for the passage of a vessel it was the duty of the platelayer to make good the road by attaching and bolting up the fishplates at each end of the bridge while the signalman re-coupled the wires. An entry showing the time of opening and closing of the bridge and 'line restored' had to be made in the train register book and signed by signalman and platelayer and until this was done the signalman was not to replace the bolt which secured the bridge and released the signals. The master of any vessel requiring to pass the bridge had to watch for three signs hoisted by the bridgeman. Initially a white flag by day or white light by night, hoisted on the flagstaff, acknowledged the vessel had been seen. If no train was due to pass over the bridge, a black ball by day or green light by night was hoisted, and finally when the span was opened a red flag by day or red light by night was hoisted. This was maintained until the bridge was about to be closed for the passage of trains. After the passing of the vessel through the channel by the bridge, the span was closed and the signal wires and fishplates replaced to allow normal railway working to commence. Langston Bridge signal box could be switched out when not required. As a precaution against damage to the bridge, Masters and pilots of vessels proceeding in either direction through Langston swing bridge were not allowed to sail through the opening but were to bring their vessels to the proper mooring buoys or piles 150 yards on either side of the bridge, one on each side of the channel and then warp their way through the bridge.

Later after 1938 to protect train working, Langston Bridge signal box was only manned when the span required to be opened and then by previous appointment. Once the 'line clear' had been given by the Hayling Island signalman to Havant for a down train and by Havant signalman to Hayling Island for an up train or when a train was running on the branch from Havant to Hayling Island or return, the bridge span could not be opened. It was permissible, however, to open the span after a down train, fitted with continuous brakes, had cleared the bridge in the direction of Hayling Island and then only after the driver and guard had been advised by the Langston Bridge signalman of what action was taking place. Langston Bridge signal box closed on 17th September, 1963 when all associated signal arms were removed.

If a breakdown or mishap occurred whilst a train was between Langston Bridge and Hayling Island the Train Staff and Ticket regulations were observed and if it was necessary for an assisting locomotive or train to approach the bridge the driver of that locomotive or train had to first ascertain that the bridge span was closed and locked.

From an operating viewpoint the 4 miles 45 chains single line track proved to be a problem during the summer season, especially from the 1930s onwards, when it was essential to move many passengers quickly and without undue delay. In the absence of passing loops it was only possible to run a regular service at 30 minute intervals, the maximum permissible headway capacity on the branch. In practice the maximum service of 24 round trips on Saturdays and 20 on Sundays was only accomplished by the use of two trains, one leaving Hayling Island as soon as the other train had arrived from Havant, with necessary shunting movements taking place within station limits before the first train arrived back at Hayling Island. Similarly on arrival at Havant, passengers had to be set down and picked up, engine watered and run round its train, all within the five minutes allowed. When passengers conveyed more than the average number of suitcases or prams and pushchairs this allowance was frequently exceeded. For many years after Grouping until the outbreak of World War II three engines were allocated to the branch on summer Saturdays so that two worked the services and the third was changeover

Langston Bridge signal box and 50 ft opening swing section from the north facing towards Hayling Island on 29th October, 1962. The signal box located on the east or down side of the structure contained a 7-lever LBSCR Tappet frame with 5 in. centres with six working and one spare lever. The signalman was also responsible for the opening and closing of the swing span with the assistance of permanent way staff. *Ken Paye*

Langston Bridge signal box located on the down side of the branch 1 mile 912 yards from Havant signal box and the 50 ft opening span in the foreground - view facing north towards Havant in October 1962. *Ken Paye*

The minute Hayling Island signal box measuring 6 ft by 6 ft located at the end of the platform with the signalmen's messroom or lobby to the right. The Tyer's one wire two position block instruments used in conjunction with Train Staff and Ticket method of single line working were accommodated in the signalmen's messroom.   *J. Johnson*

The 10-lever LBSCR Tappet frame with 5 in. centres, located in Hayling Island signal box with lever No. 7 being push or pull controlling the ground signals into and out of the goods yard.
Author's Collection

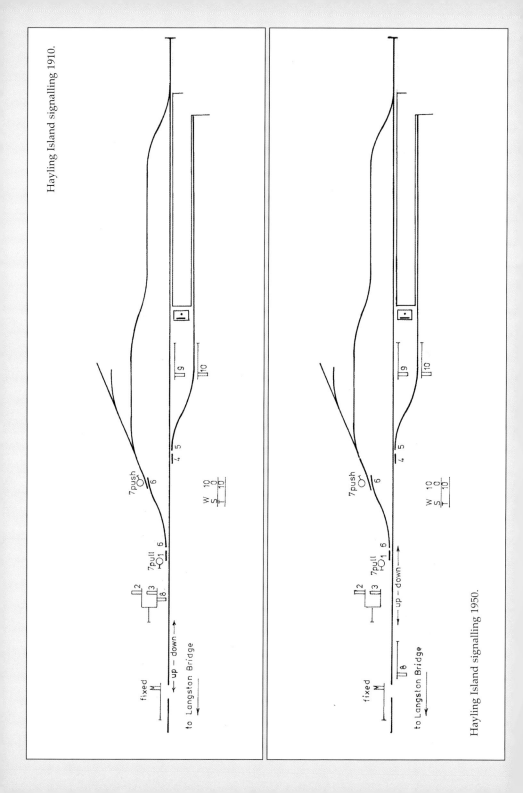

Hayling Island signalling 1910.

Hayling Island signalling 1950.

engine thus ensuring short turn round times. This was repeated in the post-war years.

Double-heading on the line was prohibited because of the weight restriction on Langston bridge (an instruction that was on some occasions ignored by engine crews). Passenger, parcels and empty stock trains, but not mixed trains, could however be assisted in the rear by a second locomotive and this method of working was compulsory when through trains, especially return excursions, ran from Hayling Island to destinations beyond Havant. On arrival of the train at Havant branch home signal the leading engine was detached and ran to the down bay platform line. The engine, which was to take the train forward, was then attached and after the detaching of the assisting engine in the rear, the train continued its journey.

Engineers' trains serving the siding at Langston were propelled from Havant and restricted to not more than eight 4-wheel or four bogie vehicles loaded or empty with an appropriate brake van in the lead. The complete train or an engine returning light to Havant was protected in accordance with the Train Staff and Ticket regulations.

Before Grouping in 1923 the last vehicle on all branch trains carried a board bearing the letters 'LV' on the near side lamp bracket by day to denote the train was complete. If a special train was to follow the last vehicle on the train carried an 'LV' board on the near side bracket and a board denoting special on the opposite bracket. By night an illuminated tail lamp was carried on the near side lamp bracket of the last vehicle if no following special train was expected whilst two tail lamps, one on the near side lamp bracket and one on the centre iron was carried if a special train was to follow. This procedure was followed even if a train was to run in the opposite direction before the passing of the special train.

In LBSCR days the maintenance of electrical apparatus and wires between Havant Junction and Hayling Island was carried out by the electric lineman's depot at Fratton under the district inspector based at Horsham, whilst signals and locking gear were the responsibility of the signal lineman's depot at Chichester under the depot inspector at Brighton. In the latter years signal & telegraph lineman Edward Goodland and assistant Henry Tannadine were responsible for signal and telecommunications over the entire branch.

Traffic Staff

In 1891 station master Mitchell was at South Hayling with responsibility for Langston and North Hayling but the following year station master Charles had assumed responsibility. Station master E. Edwards was in charge of Havant and the branch stations in 1956 whilst E.G.H. Clarke was at Havant prior to closure of branch.

Traffic staff at Havant in the last years included porters Gibbard, Nash, Grout, Budd, Cherrison, Clarke, Baldwin, Bryden, Ware, parcels clerk Ousley, booking clerk Craswell, booking clerk Willmott, ticket collector Evans, and foreman Les Horwood. In Havant signal box were signalmen Harry Griffin and signal lad Michael Prior on one shift.

In the 1920s Ellen (Nell) Charman, the wife of local milkman James Charman, was employed as gatekeeper at Langston crossing. They lived in No. 1 Railway Cottages close to the railway. Others serving at Langston crossing included Albert Grout, Jack Dalton, crossing keeper, O'Shea who also worked as a taxi driver, and relief crossing keeper Prior.

Of the staff at Hayling Island in World War I, Mabel Crasweller was employed as lady porter and travelled daily to North Hayling to tidy the station and clean out the waiting shed. In the latter years four staff were ex-military men and consequently the station was known locally as the barracks; Doug 'Sweeney' Todd, an ex-Royal Marine, whose motor cycle was a regular feature at the end of Hayling Island platform was once asked why he never travelled by train to and from work. He advised that as signalman on early turn he had to open the signal box and clear the line for the arrival of the first train from Havant and that on late turn after the departure of the last train he had to advise Havant that the train had left and then close the line for the night. He opined that being a signalman at the end of the line was no easy task, for from signalling a train into the platform and arranging for the engine to run-round the stock and depart for Havant required 36 movements of levers in the signal box. No one dared argue with him! Others included porters Ray Woolgar, and Ripsher, Evans, Nash and relief signalman Herbert Brook.

Samuel Walder, who joined the LBSCR as a lad porter at Havant, was promoted to guard on the Hayling Island branch in 1899 and worked the line until retirement in 1934. During World War II the SR employed many female guards including Molly Smith who worked regularly on the branch. Guards on the line at the time of closure included Instrall and Frederick Norris who had started his railway career at Havant as a signal box lad. He was the Hayling branch guard from 1953 to 1963 and recalled Whitsun 1961 when approximately 568 passengers were packed into a three-coach train en route to the coast!

A study of staff at Hayling Island in the early 1900s includes station master, two porters and booking clerk. The station was a popular destination for homing pigeons traffic and the sack truck is loaded with two baskets of the precious cargo released or about to be released. *Author's Collection*

Chapter Seven

Timetables and Traffic

The initial timetable for the line showed Furniss working six trains in each direction, on weekdays only, for the Hayling company. Down trains departed Havant at 7.10, 8.20, 11.40 am, 2.22, 4.00 and 6.30 pm, whilst up trains departed Hayling Island at 7.35, 10.10 am, 12.10, 2.54, 5.00 and 7.20 pm. Calls were made at Langstone and North Hayling by request only, and trains were allowed 20 minutes for the journey. By February 1868 this ambitious timetable had been reduced to four trains each way with departures from Havant at 8.20, 11.00 am, 2.22 and 4.00 pm, returning from Hayling Island at 10.05 am, 12.10, 2.50 and 4.35 pm weekdays only. Calls at Langstone and North Hayling were by request only. The line was closed to traffic from December 1868 until services resumed in August 1869, when Hayling Island station was retitled South Hayling.

When the LBSCR took over the branch in 1872, the company retained the service of four weekday trains in each direction with slightly altered timings. Trains departed Havant at 8.45, 10.30 am, 12.00 noon and 4.40 pm, returning from South Hayling at 9.05, 11.20 am, 1.25 and 5.00 pm, whilst the overall journey time was reduced to 15 minutes for the 4 miles 45 chains journey. By 1880 the journey time was again extended to 20 minutes, although the service had increased to seven trains in each direction, on weekdays only. The branch was worked from the South Hayling end of the line after the establishment of the engine shed at the terminus in 1874 and up services departed South Hayling at 8.10, 9.50, 11.00 am, 1.20, 3.20, 4.40 and 5.50 pm, returning from Havant at 9.20, 10.30, 11.55 am, 2.00, 4.05, 5.05 pm (Tuesdays and Saturdays only), 6.20 and 7.35 pm.

By 1890 the following branch service was offered weekdays only with connections from and to Portsmouth Town.

Up		am	am	am	pm	pm	pm	pm
South Hayling	dep.	8.05	9.45	10.55	1.20	3.10	4.40	6.55
North Hayling	dep.	8.12	9.52	11.02	1.27	3.17	4.47	7.02
Langston	dep.	8.19	9.59	11.09	1.34	3.24	4.54	7.09
Havant	arr.	8.25	10.05	11.15	1.40	3.30	5.00	7.15
Portsmouth Town	arr.	9.25	10.40	12.02	2.16	4.23	5.44	7.33

Down		am	am	am	pm	pm	pm	pm
Portsmouth Town	dep.	9.00	9.55	11.35	1.25	3.25	4.45	7.15
Havant	dep.	9.20	10.30	11.55	2.05	4.10	6.25	7.35
Langston	dep.	9.24	10.34	11.59	2.09	4.14	6.29	7.39
North Hayling	dep.	9.31	10.41	12.06	2.16	4.21	6.36	7.46
South Hayling	arr.	9.40	10.50	12.15	2.25	4.30	6.45	7.55

From 1st June, 1892 South Hayling station reverted to being titled Hayling Island and two years later in 1894 Hayling Island engine shed was closed; thereafter the line was worked from the Havant end. Near the turn of the century the services had again increased to 10 trains each way on weekdays and seven in each direction on Sundays. The 1898 summer timetable showed trains departing Havant on weekdays at 7.15, 9.20, 10.30, 11.55 am, 12.58, 2.05, 3.45, 5.10, 6.25 and 7.35 pm, returning from Hayling Island at 7.55, 9.45, 10.55 am, 12.25, 1.23, 2.45, 4.37, 5.37, 6.55 and 8.15 pm. On Sundays down trains departed Havant at 9.40, 11.35 am, 2.50, 4.10, 6.26, 7.40 and

9.00 pm, whilst up departures from Hayling Island left at 10.30 am, 2.26, 3.40, 5.30, 7.05, 8.30 and 9.30 pm, the latter running non-stop to Havant in 10 minutes.

The journey times from London to Hayling Island varied considerably in 1909 from 2 hours 56 mins in the up direction and three hours in the down direction by the LSWR Portsmouth direct line to and from Waterloo, compared to 2 hours 48 mins down and 2 hours 25 mins in the up direction to and from Victoria by the LBSCR Mid-Sussex line.

In October 1910 the weekdays-only winter train service of LBSCR motor trains offering one class only departed Havant at 8.20, 9.17, 10.33 am 12.00 noon, 12.58, 1.50, 4.25, 5.20, 6.25, 7.35 and 9.20 pm returning from Hayling Island at 8.50, 9.37, 10.53 am, 12.30, 1.20, 2.55, 4.45, 5.50, 7.00, 8.35 and 9.45 pm. Fifteen minutes running time was allowed across the branch.

The timetable commencing June 1912 offered the following service:

Down

Weekdays		am	am	am	pm	noon	pm	pm
Havant	dep.	7.25	8.20	9.17	10.33	12.00	12.58	2.12
Langston	dep.	7.29	8.24	9.21	10.37	12.04	1.02	2.16
North Hayling	dep.	7.35	8.30	9.27	10.43	12.10	1.08	2.22
Hayling Island	arr.	7.40	8.35	9.32	10.48	12.15	1.13	2.27

| | pm | pm | pm | pm | pm | pm
---|---|---|---|---|---|---|---
Havant | dep. | 3.37 | 4.20 | 5.20 | 6.25 | 7.40 | 9.20
Langston | dep. | 3.41 | 4.24 | 5.24 | 6.29 | 7.44 | 9.24
North Hayling | dep. | 3.47 | 4.30 | 5.30 | 6.35 | 7.50 | 9.30
Hayling Island | arr. | 3.52 | 4.35 | 5.35 | 6.40 | 7.55 | 9.35

| | | | | B | | |
---|---|---|---|---|---|---|---|---
Sundays | | am | am | pm | pm | pm | pm | pm
Havant | dep. | 9.30 | 11.40 | 2.50 | 4.10 | 6.15 | 7.45 | 9.00
Langston | dep. | 9.34 | 11.44 | 2.54 | 4.14 | 6.19 | 7.49 | 9.04
North Hayling | dep. | 9.40 | 11.50 | 3.00 | 4.20 | 6.25 | 7.55 | 9.10
Hayling Island | arr. | 9.45 | 11.55 | 3.05 | 4.25 | 6.30 | 8.00 | 9.15

Up

| | | | | | | | A
---|---|---|---|---|---|---|---|---
Weekdays | | am | am | am | am | pm | pm | pm
Hayling Island | dep. | 7.55 | 8.40 | 9.37 | 10.53 | 12.25 | 1.20 | 2.55
North Hayling | dep. | 8.00 | 8.45 | 9.42 | 10.58 | 12.30 | 1.25 | 3.00
Langston | dep. | 8.06 | 8.51 | 9.48 | 11.04 | 12.36 | 1.31 | 3.06
Havant | arr. | 8.10 | 8.55 | 9.52 | 11.08 | 12.40 | 1.35 | 3.10

| | B | | | | | |
---|---|---|---|---|---|---|---|---
| | pm | pm | pm | pm | pm | pm | pm
Hayling Island | dep. | 3.05 | 4.00 | 4.45 | 5.50 | 7.00 | 8.28 | 9.45
North Hayling | dep. | 3.10 | 4.05 | 4.50 | 5.55 | 7.05 | 8.33 | 9.50
Langston | dep. | 3.16 | 4.11 | 4.56 | 6.01 | 7.11 | 8.39 | 9.56
Havant | arr. | 3.20 | 4.15 | 5.00 | 6.05 | 7.15 | 8.43 | 10.00

| | | | B | | | |
---|---|---|---|---|---|---|---|---
Sundays | | am | pm | pm | pm | pm | pm | pm
Hayling Island | dep. | 10.35 | 2.25 | 3.45 | 5.30 | 7.10 | 8.10 | 9.25
North Hayling | dep. | 10.40 | 2.30 | 3.50 | 5.35 | 7.15 | 8.15 | 9.30
Langston | dep. | 10.46 | 2.36 | 3.56 | 5.41 | 7.21 | 8.21 | 9.36
Havant | arr. | 10.50 | 2.40 | 4.00 | 5.45 | 7.25 | 8.25 | 9.40

A – June only, B - Commences July

During the last year of LBSCR operation, the service had not altered dramatically and the working timetable for October 1922 showed 12 weekday departures from Havant at 7.00 ECS,* 7.50, 8.50 mixed, 10.30, 11.20 am, 12.50, 1.58, 4.20, 5.42, 6.30, 7.40 and 9.18 pm. In the up direction 12 weekday trains departed Hayling Island at 7.18, 8.16, 9.25, 10.52 am, 12.25, 1.20, 3.00 mixed, 4.50, 6.05, 6.55, 8.15 and 9.42 pm. The last trains in each direction ran on Wednesdays and Saturdays only after October. On Sundays down services departed Havant at 10.00 am, 12.00 noon, 2.30, 4.00, 6.30 and 7.45 pm returning from Hayling Island at 10.40 am, 2.00, 3.15, 5.40, 7.10 and 8.30 pm, the latter a through train to Portsmouth. Mixed trains conveyed all goods traffic.

The SR made few initial changes to the services and the timetable for 1924 showed 15 down weekday departures from Havant at 7.00, 7.39, 8.32, 9.20, 10.28 am, 12.08, 1.05, 1.55 SX, 2.07 SO, 3.03, 4.30 SX, 4.45 SO, 5.42, 6.50, 7.38, 8.23 and 9.18 pm; returning from Hayling Island at 7.17, 8.01, 8.54, 10.05, 10.50 am, 12.35, 1.27, 2.40, 3.25, 4.58, 6.05, 7.13, 8.00, 8.45 and 9.42 pm. The 7.00 down and 10.05 up trains were non-stop services and allowed 10 minutes running time, whilst all other services called at all stations and were allowed 15 minutes for the 4 miles 45 chains journey.

Four years later the timetable operative from 25th March, 1928 showed the following weekday service from Havant; 6.55, 7.33, 8.31, 9.20, 10.38, 11.30 am, 12.55, 1.52, 3.03, 4.33, 5.36, 6.15 SX, 6.54, 7.42, 8.26 SX, 8.38 SO and 9.25 pm. The return workings from Hayling Island departed at 7.12, 7.55, 8.54, 10.10, 10.59 am, 12.11, 1.21, 2.40, 3.30, 5.08, 5.57 SX, 6.25 SO, 6.33 SX, 7.15, 8.03, 8.50 SX, 8.59 SO and 9.59 pm. The 6.55 am and 6.15 pm SX down trains and the 5.57 pm SX up service ran non-stop between Havant and Hayling Island and were allowed 10 minutes running time. All other services called at the intermediate stations and were allowed 14 minutes except the 9.20 am ex-Havant and the 3.30 pm ex-Hayling Island, which were mixed trains and were allowed 15 and 17 minutes respectively. On Sundays trains departed Havant at 9.24, 10.07, 11.30 am, 12.48, 2.32, 3.50, 6.54 and 7.42 pm returning from Hayling Island at 9.45, 10.28, 11.55 am, 1.55, 3.15, 6.00, 7.10 and 8.30 pm, all trains being allowed 14 minutes.

The working timetable operative from 6th July, 1930 showed a service of 16 passenger and one mixed trains in the down direction Mondays to Fridays with an additional late passenger train departing from Havant at 11.49 pm on Wednesdays only, with an equivalent number in the up direction, save that the additional 12.06 am ex-Hayling Island on Thursdays only was ECS to Portsmouth. On Saturdays 15 passenger trains and one mixed train ran each way and on Sundays a service of 10 passenger trains each way was provided. All passenger trains called at all stations and were allowed 14 minutes, except the first down train 6.50 am ex-Havant ECS which omitted the intermediate stops and was allowed 20 minutes. The mixed trains 9.20 am ex-Havant and 1.21 pm SO and 3.43 pm SX ex-Hayling Island were permitted 15 minutes running time.

The popularity of Hayling Island as a holiday centre can be gauged by the high summer weekday service provided from 18th July, 1932 when 14 minutes continued to be allowed for the journey. Down trains departed Havant at 6.45, 7.24, 8.31, 9.30 mixed, 10.30, 11.20 am, 12.15 SO, 12.17 SX, 12.55 SO, 1.00 SX, 1.53, 2.52 SO, 3.17 SX, 4.30, 5.22 SX, 5.37 SO, 6.10 SX, 6.50 SO, 6.54 SX, 7.35, 8.28, 9.38 and 11.55 pm WO. Return services departed from Hayling Island at 7.02, 7.44, 8.52, 9.58am, 10.51, 11.50 SO, 11.56 am SX, 12.54 SO, 12.58 SX, 1.16 SO, 1.21 SX, 2.15 SO, 2.44 SX, 3.44 SO, 3.48 SX, 4.51, 5.49 SX, 6.05 SO 6.31 SX, 7.11 SO, 7.15 SX, 7.58, 8.49, 9.51 pm and 12.13 am ECS on Thursdays only to Portsmouth. On Sundays 10 trains ran in each direction commencing with the 7.07 am ex-Havant and finishing with the 8.46 pm ex-Hayling Island.

---

* Timetable abbreviations used: ECS - empty coaching stock, SO - Saturdays only, SX-Saturdays excepted, WO - Wednesdays only, WSO - Wednesdays and Saturdays only.

HAVANT AND HAYLING ISLAND.

JULY 6th to SEPTEMBER 21st only.

DOWN TRAINS. WEEK DAYS.

Distance m.c.		Pas	Pas	Pas	M'd	Pas	Pas	Pas	Pas	Pas	Pas	Pas	Pas	Pas	SONS Pas	SONS Pas	SONS Pas	SONS Pas	NS Pas	Pas	Pas	WO Pas
...	Havant............dep.	a.m. 8 50	a.m. 7 28	a.m. 8 31	a.m. 9 20	a.m. 10 32	a.m. 11 16	a.m. 11 17	p.m. 12 59	p.m. 1 0	p.m. 1 7	p.m. 1 23	p.m. 3 10	p.m. 3 24	p.m. 3 35	p.m. 3 6 16	p.m. 6 56 7	p.m. 7 42	p.m. 8 28	p.m. 9 28	p.m. ...	p.m. 11 48
1 9	Langston............ "	...	7 32	8 39	9 24	10 36	11 20	11 21	1 3	1 4	1 10	...	3 14	3 28	3 39	5 6 40	7 0 7	7 46	8 32	9 33	...	11 52
3 30	North Hayling...... "	...	7 38	8 41	9 30	10 42	11 26	11 27	1 9	1 10	2 3	2 20	3 20	3 27	4 4	5 46 24	7 6 7	7 52	8 38	9 39	...	11 58
4 45	Hayling Island...arr.	7 0 7	7 42	8 45	9 35	10 46	11 30	11 31	1 13	1 14	2 8	2 43	3 24	3 31	4 16	4 6 28	7 10 7	7 58	8 42	9 43	...	12 2

UP TRAINS. WEEK DAYS.

Distance m.c.		Pas	Pas	Pas	Pas	Pas	Pas	Pas	SO Pas	NS Pas	Mxd	Pas	Pas	SO Pas	NS Pas	SONS Fre	SONS Pas	SONS Pas	Mxd	Pas	Pas	Pas	Pas	Pas	WO Mgt.
...	Hayling Island...dep.	a.m. 7 7	a.m. 7 17	a.m. 7 49	a.m. 8 52	a.m. 10 4	a.m. 10 53	a.m. 11 56	p.m. 12 38	p.m. 12 42	p.m. 1 21	p.m. 1 21	p.m. 2 0	p.m. 2 40	p.m. 3 1	p.m. 4 03	p.m. 4 3	p.m. 5 35	p.m. 5 57	p.m. 6 0	p.m. 6 35	p.m. 7 17	p.m. 8 3	p.m. 8 50	p.m. 12 6
0 9	North Hayling...... "	7 11	7 21	8 53	8 56	10 8	10 57	12 0	12 41	12 42	2 81	2 88	2 4	2 43	3 3	4 13	4 7	5 4	6 0	6 4	6 39	7 21	8 6	8 54	...
3 30	Langston............ "	7 17	7 17	5 9 9	2 10 1	10 14	11 3	12 6	12 48	1 3	3 02	5 09	8	5 15	4 10	4 50	5	5 15	6 6	6 10	6 45	7 27	8 18	9 0	0 10
4 45	Havant............arr.	7 21	7 21	8 3 9	6 10 18	11 7	11 10	12 52	1 38	1 35	3 42	5 43	4 54	5	5 19	6	6 14	6 49	7 31	8 17	9 4	4 10 0	4 10 4	...	12 16

SUNDAYS.

DOWN TRAINS. SUNDAYS.

m.c.		Pas	Pas	Pas	Pas	Pas	Pas	Pas	Pas	Pas	Pas
	Havant............dep.	a.m. 9 7	a.m. 9 55	a.m. 10 49	a.m. 11 50	p.m. 12 50	p.m. 2 30	p.m. 3 5	p.m. 5 20	p.m. 6 30	p.m. 7 53
	Langston............	9 11	9 59	10 53	11 54	12 54	2 34	3 9	5 24	6 34	7 57
	North Hayling......	9 17	10 5	10 59	12 0	2 40	2 40	3 15	5 30	6 40	8 2
	Hayling Island...arr.	9 21	10 9	11 3	12 41	1 2	2 44	3 45	5 34	6 44	8 7

UP TRAINS. SUNDAYS.

		Pas	Pas	Pas	Pas	Pas	Pas	Pas	Pas	Pas	Pas
	Hayling Island...dep.	a.m. 9 28	a.m. 10 16	a.m. 11 10	p.m. 12 12	p.m. 1 50	p.m. 3 15	p.m. 4 35	p.m. 6 7	p.m. 8 40
	North Hayling...... "	9 32	10 20	11 14	12 16	1 54	3 19	4 39	6 11	8 44
	Langston............ "	9 38	10 26	11 20	12 22	2 0	3 25	4 45	6 17	8 50
	Havant............arr.	9 42	10 30	11 24	12 26	2 4	3 29	4 49	6 21	8 54

SR working timetable 1930.

By 1935 the winter timetable offered 17 trains each way SX and 16 SO. Havant departures were 6.42, 7.23, 8.20, 9.20, 10.24, 11.16 am, 12.02, 12.46, 1.51, 2.50 SO, 3.18 SX, 4.21, 5.25, 6.09, 6.53, 7.37, 8.27 and 9.30 pm. Up trains departed Hayling Island at 7.00, 7.44, 8.50, 9.56, 10.46, 11.39 am, 12.23, 1.07, 2.13 SO, 2.43 SX, 3.39 SO, 3.45 SX, 4.43, 5.46, 6.31 SX, 7.15, 8.01, 8.49 and 9.56 pm. Running times were extended to 15 minutes except for the 6.42 am ex-Havant which ran non-stop to Hayling Island in 11 minutes. The mixed trains were allowed additional running time, the 8.20 am ex-Havant 16 minutes and the 2.42 pm ex-Hayling Island 17 minutes, to allow for the extra loading of goods wagons and any additional shunting required at Langston. Sunday services resumed on and from 5th May, 1935 with 12 trains in each direction, all with 15 minutes timing. Down departures from Havant were 9.05, 9.58, 10.47, 11.45 am, 1.00, 2.03, 2.58, 3.51, 5.15, 6.35, 7.43 and 8.27 pm, with up trains returning from Hayling Island at 9.35, 10.19, 11.08 am, 12.15, 1.40, 2.30, 3.19, 4.13, 6.05, 7.05, 8.05 and 9.00 pm.

After Grouping, London traffic was directed to and from Waterloo, and the average timings after World War II were 1 hour 58 minutes down and 1 hour 41 minutes in the up direction, the vast improvement originally dating from the electrification of the Portsmouth direct line in July 1937.

On the outbreak of World War II in September 1939 the following service was operating: departing Havant at 6.35 non-stop to Hayling Island, 7.20 mixed, 8.16, 9.07 mixed, 10.19, 11.19 am, 12.06, 12.50, 1.34, 2.20, 3.53, 4.37, 5.33, 6.20, 7.20, 8.20, 9.47 and 10.47 pm WSO. In the up direction trains departed Hayling Island at 6.58, 7.46, 8.40, 9.52, 10.52, 11.45 am, 12.27, 1.12, 1.57, 3.20 mixed, 4.16, 5.06, 5.57, 6.52, 7.52, 8.49, 10.10 and 11.07 pm WSO. On Sundays 15 trains ran in each direction including the non-stop 6.16 pm ex-Havant.

By October 1940 the service had been slightly reduced to 15 trains each way SX and 16 SO and no Sunday service. Trains departed Havant at 6.35, 7.17, 8.16, 9.07, 10.19, 11.19 am, 12.06, 12.50, 1.34, 2.20 SO, 3.53, 4.37, 5.33, 6.20 SX, 6.34 SO, 7.20 SX, 7.34 SO, 8.20 SX and 8.34 pm SO and returning from Hayling Island at 6.58, 7.46, 8.40, 9.52, 10.52, 11.45 am, 12.27, 1.12, 1.57 SO, 3.18, 4.16, 5.06, 5.57, 6.52, 7.52 and 8.52 pm. All train timings were accelerated to 13 minutes, with the exception of the 6.35 down train which ran non-stop to Hayling Island in 10 minutes and the 9.07 am ex-Havant mixed train which omitted calling at North Hayling and was timed for 14 minutes. The up mixed train 3.18 pm ex-Hayling Island called at all stations and had a 17 minutes timing to Havant.

Because of Hayling Island's strategic position, branch traffic was not reduced drastically during hostilities. The March 1942 timetable showed a marked similarity to previous years with Havant departures at 6.35 am non-stop to Hayling Island, 7.17, 8.16, 9.07, 10.19, 11.19 am, 12.00 noon, 12.50, 1.34, 2.20 SO, 3.53, 4.37, 5.33, 6.20 SX, 6.34 SO, 7.20 SX, 7.34 SO, 8.20 SX and 8.34 pm SO. Up trains departed Hayling Island at 6.58, 7.46, 8.40, 9.52, 10.52, 11.45 am, 12.21, 1.12, 1.57 SO, 3.18, 4.16, 5.09, 5.57, 6.52, 7.52 and 8.52 pm. The timetable for 1944 was very similar with only minor timing alterations. In the down direction the 12.00 noon train departed six minutes later, whilst the 12.21 pm departed at 12.27 and the 5.09 pm at 5.06. The 9.07 am down and the 3.18 pm up services ran as mixed trains.

The last summer service operated by the Southern Railway (1947) showed 15 trains each way SX with 16 SO and 9 in each direction on Sundays. Down weekday trains departed Havant at 6.35, 7.17, 8.16, 9.07, 10.19, 11.19 am, 12.06, 12.50, 1.34, 2.20pm SO, 3.53, 4.37, 5.33, 6.20 SX, 6.34 SO, 7.20 SX, 7.34 SO, 8.20 SX and 8.34 pm SO returning from Hayling Island at 6.58, 7.46, 8.40, 9.45, 10.52, 11.45 am, 12.27, 1.12,

SR 'A1X' class 0-6-0T No. 2644 wends its way around the 19 chains radius curves near Havant with her two-coach train formed of short wheelbase ex-LSWR non-gangway brake composite and brake third, en route to Hayling Island in the spring of 1938. The locomotive was built in June 1877 as class 'A1' and entered traffic as LBSCR No. 44 *Fulham* and was later transferred to the duplicate stock as No. 644 being rebuilt as class 'A1X' in 1912. On takeover by the SR she became No. B644 and then 2644 and after nationalization No. 32644 before being withdrawn in April 1951.   *C.R.L. Coles*

Displaying the wrong headcode for the branch, 'A1X' class 0-6-0T No. 32677 works the single-coach 2.35 pm Havant to Hayling Island train near East Street overbridge No. 1 on 3rd May, 1953. Formerly LBSCR No. 77 *Wonersh*, the engine was transferred to the Isle of Wight where it became SR No. W3 and later W13 *Carisbrooke*. It returned to the mainland in 1949 bearing SR malachite green livery to work on the Hayling Island branch complete with new number but minus nameplates, which had been transferred to 'O2' class 0-4-4T No. 36 on the Isle of Wight. Although one carriage sufficed for normal weekday autumn, winter and early spring services, two coaches were utilized on Tuesdays (Havant market day).   *LCGB/Ken Nunn Collection*

1.57 SO, 3.18 SX, 3.22 SO, 4.16, 5.06, 5.57, 6.52, 7.52 and 8.52 pm. Sunday services departed Havant at 10.35 am and then hourly at 35 minutes past each hour until 7.35 pm, with the exception of the 4.35 pm. Up services departed Hayling Island at hourly intervals between 10.55 am and 7.55 pm, with the exception of the 3.55 pm. All trains called at all stations and were allowed 13 minutes running time. The exceptions were the 6.35 am down train which ran non-stop to Hayling Island in 10 minutes, the 9.07 am mixed ex-Havant and the 6.58 am ex-Hayling Island with a 15 minute timing, and the 3.18 pm SX up which ran as a mixed train with a 17 minute timing. Sunday services were curtailed after 21st September and from 6th October the weekday services was reduced to 12 trains SX and 13 SO in each direction.

By 1948 the Southern Railway had succumbed to the nationalized British Railways Southern Region but winter services remained almost as before. Down departures from Havant left at 6.35, by now omitting North Hayling only, 7.17, 8.16, 9.07, 10.19 am, 12.50, 1.34, 2.20 SO, 4.42, 5.33, 6.20 SX, 6.34 SO, 7.29 SX, 7.34 SO, 8.20 SX and 8.34 pm SO. Hayling Island departures were at 6.58, 7.46, 8.40, 9.45 am, 12.27, 1.12, 1.57 SO, 2.18 SX, 3.22 SO, 5.06, 5.57, 6.52, 7.52 and 8.58 pm.

The summer timetable operative from 30th June to 14th September, 1952 showed 14 SX and 17 SO trains each way on weekdays and nine in each direction on Sundays. Down weekday trains departed Havant at 6.35, 7.34, 8.20, 9.12, 10.10 SO, 10.19 SX, 10.55 SO, 11.19 SX, 11.53 am SO, 12.35, 1.17 SO, 1.34 SX, 1.59 SO, 2.53 SO, 3.34 SX, 4.05 SO, 4.42 SX, 4.52 SO, 5.33, 6.20 SX, 6.34 SO, 7.20 SX, 7.34 SO, 8.20 SX and 8.34 pm SO. Trains returned from Hayling Island at 7.07, 8.00, 8.40, 9.45 SX, 9.48 SO, 10.32 SO, 10.52 SX, 11.32 SO, 11.55 am SX, 12.14 SO, 12.55, 1.38 SO, 2.20 SO, 2.53 SX, 3.30 SO, 4.16 SX, 4.26 SO, 5.06 SX, 5.13 SO, 5.57, 6.52, 7.52 and 8.52 pm. Sunday services were unchanged from those operated in 1947. All trains called at all stations and were allowed 13 minutes running time on the branch with the weekday exceptions of the 6.35 am ex-Havant which omitted North Hayling and was allowed 10 minutes, whilst the 9.12 am and 12.35 pm down services ran as mixed trains with 16 and 14 minute timings respectively. In the up direction the 8.00 am and 2.53 pm SX ran as mixed trains with 15 and 17 minute timings respectively.

The high summer service of 1958 again emphasised the popularity of Hayling Island as a holiday resort and the interval service on Saturdays gave a reflection of the number of passengers carried, which often exceeded 7,000 in one day. Havant departures on Mondays to Fridays were 6.30 mixed omitting North Hayling, 7.34, 8.15, 9.12 mixed, 10.35, 11.35 am, 12.35, 1.35, 2.20, 3.35, 4.42, 5.33, 6.20, 7.20 and 8.34 pm. In the up direction Monday to Friday services departed Hayling Island at 7.02, 7.55, 8.35, 9.45, 10.55, 11.55 am, 12.55, 1.55, 2.53 mixed, 4.16, 5.06, 5.57, 6.47, 7.52 and 8.52 pm. Saturday down departures from Havant were 6.30 mixed omitting North Hayling, 7.34, 8.15, 9.12 mixed, 10.05, 10.35*, 11.05, 11.35* am, 12.05, 12.35, 1.05, 1.35*, 2.05, 2.35*, 3.05, 3.35*, 4.05, 4.35*, 5.05, 5.35*, 6.05, 6.35, 7.35 and 8.34 pm. Saturday departures from Hayling Island were 7.02, 7.55, 8.35, 9.45, 10.20*, 10.47, 11.20*, 11.47 am, 12.20*, 12.47, 1.20*, 1.47, 2.20*, 2.47, 3.20*, 3.47, 4.20*, 4.47, 5.20*, 5.47, 6.20*, 6.49, 7.17, 7.53 and 8.52pm. For Sunday travellers trains departed Havant at 10.05, 10.35*, 11.05, 11.35* am, 12.05, 12.35*, 1.05, 1.35*, 2.05, 2.35, 3.05, 3.35*, 4.05, 4.35*, 5.05, 5.35*, 6.05, 6.35*, 7.05, 7.35* and 8.05 pm. Up trains departed from Hayling Island at 10.47, 11.20*, 11.47 am, 12.20*, 12.47, 1.20*, 1.47, 2.20*, 2.47, 3.20*, 3.47, 4.20*, 4.47, 5.20*, 5.47, 6.20*, 6.47, 7.20*, 7.47 and 8.20 pm. Stopping trains were allowed 13 minutes running time and non-stop services 10 minutes.

The final timetable from September 1963 allowed trains 13 minutes for the journey with down departures from Havant at 6.30 omitting North Hayling, 7.34, 8.15, 9.12,

---

* Non-stop service.

These timings **WILL NOT APPLY ON SATURDAYS**, 22nd June to 14th September, 1957

DOWN WEEKDAYS

Mileage M	Mileage C			Mixed am	am	am	Mixed am	am Commences 14th Sept.	am Until 13th September inclusive		am	PM	PM
0	0	**HAVANT** .. .. (SD) dep	1	6 35	7 34	8 15	9 12	10 19	10 35	..	11 35	12 35	1 35
1	14	Langston ....(B)....	2	6 39	7 37½	8 18½	9 16	10 22½	10 38½	......	11 38½	12 38½	1 38½
2	40	North Hayling	3	..	7 42	8 23	9 23	10 27	10 43	..	11 43	12 43	1 43
4	50	**HAYLING ISLAND** (SD) arr	4	6 48	7 47	8 28	9 28	10 32	10 48	......	11 48	12 48	1 48

DOWN WEEKDAYS

			SO PM	PM	PM	PM		SX PM	SO PM		SX PM	SO PM	SX PM Until 13th September inclusive	SX PM Commences 16th September	SO PM
HAVANT .. .. .. dep	1	..	2 20	3 35	4 42	5 33	..	6 20	6 34	..	7 20	7 34	8 34	8 20	8 34
Langston	2	......	2 23½	3 38½	4 45½	5 36½	......	6 23½	6 37½	......	7 23½	7 37½	8 37½	8 23½	8 37½
North Hayling	3	..	2 28	3 43	4 50	5 41	..	6 28	6 42	..	7 28	7 42	8 42	8 28	8 42
HAYLING ISLAND .. arr	4	......	2 33	3 48	4 55	5 46	......	6 33	6 47	......	7 33	7 47	8 47	8 33	8 47

These timings **WILL APPLY ON SATURDAYS**, 22nd June to 14th September, 1957

DOWN SATURDAYS

		Mixed am	am	am	Mixed am	am	am	am	am	PM	PM	PM	PM	PM	PM
HAVANT .. .. .. dep	1	6 35	7 34	8 15	9 12	10 5	10 35	11 5	11 35	12 5	12 35	1 5	1 35	2 5	2 35
Langston	2	6 39	7 37½	8 18½	9 16	10 8½	......	11 8½	......	12 8½	......	1 8½	......	2 8½	......
North Hayling	3	..	7 42	8 23	9 23	10 13	..	11 13	..	12 13	..	1 13	..	2 13	..
HAYLING ISLAND .. arr	4	6 48	7 47	8 28	9 28	10 18	10 45	11 18	11 45	12 18	12 45	1 18	1 45	2 18	2 45

DOWN SATURDAYS

		PM	PM	PM	PM	PM	PM	PM	PM	PM	PM				
HAVANT .. .. .. dep	1	3 5	3 35	4 5	4 35	5 5	5 35	6 5	6 35	7 35	8 34	..	..	..	..
Langston	2	3 8½	......	4 8½	......	5 8½	......	6 8½	6 38½	7 38½	8 37½	......	......	......	......
North Hayling	3	3 13	..	4 13	..	5 13	..	6 13	6 43	7 43	8 42	..	..	..	..
HAYLING ISLAND .. arr	4	3 18	3 45	4 18	4 45	5 18	5 45	6 18	6 48	7 48	8 47	......	......	......	......

These timings **WILL APPLY ON SUNDAYS**, 23rd June to 15th September, 1957

DOWN SUNDAYS

			am	am	am	am	PM	PM	PM	PM	PM	PM	PM	PM	
HAVANT .. .. .. dep	1	..	10 5	10 35	11 5	11 35	12 5	12 35	1 5	1 35	2 5	2 35	3 5	3 35	..
Langston	2	......	10 8½	......	11 8½	......	12 8½	......	1 8½	......	2 8½	......	3 8½	......	......
North Hayling	3	..	10 13	..	11 13	..	12 13	..	1 13	..	2 13	..	3 13	..	..
HAYLING ISLAND .. arr	4	......	10 18	10 45	11 18	11 45	12 18	12 45	1 18	1 45	2 18	2 45	3 18	3 45	......

DOWN SUNDAYS

			PM	PM	PM	PM	PM	PM	PM	PM	PM				
HAVANT .. .. .. dep	1	..	4 5	4 35	5 5	5 35	6 5	6 35	7 5	7 35	8 5	..	..	..	..
Langston	2	......	4 8½	......	5 8½	......	6 8½	......	7 8½	......	8 8½	......	......	......	......
North Hayling	3	..	4 13	..	5 13	..	6 13	..	7 13	..	8 13	..	..	..	..
HAYLING ISLAND .. arr	4	......	4 18	4 45	5 18	5 45	6 18	6 45	7 18	7 45	8 18	......	......	......	......

COMMENCES 27th April, 1958

DOWN SUNDAYS

		am		am		PM	PM		PM	PM		PM	PM		PM
HAVANT .. .. .. dep	1	10 35	..	11 35	..	12 35	1 35	..	2 35	3 35	..	5 35	6 35	..	7 35
Langston	2	10 38½	......	11 38½	......	12 38½	1 38½	......	2 38½	3 38½	......	5 38½	6 38½	......	7 38½
North Hayling	3	10 43	..	11 43	..	12 43	1 43	..	2 43	3 43	..	5 43	6 43	..	7 43
HAYLING ISLAND .. arr	4	10 48	......	11 48	......	12 48	1 48	......	2 48	3 48	......	5 48	6 48	......	7 48

BR (SR) working timetable for the branch (down trains), summer 1957.

A200 Hayling Island and Havant

These timings WILL NOT APPLY ON SATURDAYS, 22nd June to 14th September, 1957

UP WEEKDAYS

Mileage M	Mileage C			am	am	am	am	am Commences 16th September	am Until 13th September	am	PM		SO PM	SX PM Mixed
0	0	HAYLING ISLAND (ST) dep	1	7 2	7 55	8 35	9 45	10 52	10 55	11 55	12 55		1 55	2 53
2	10	North Hayling	2	7 7	8 0	8 40	9 50	10 57	11 0	12 0	1 0		2 0	3 0
3	36	Langston (B)	3	7 11½	8 4½	8 44½	9 54½	11 1½	11 4½	12 4½	1 4½		2 4½	3 6
4	50	HAVANT (ST) arr	4	7 15	8 8	8 48	9 58	11 5	11 8	12 8	1 8		2 8	3 10

UP WEEKDAYS

		SO PM		PM	PM		PM	SX PM Until 13th September	SX PM Commences 16th September	SO PM		PM		PM
HAYLING ISLAND .. dep	1	2 57	..	4 16	5 6	..	5 57	6 47	6 50	6 52	..	7 52	..	8 52
North Hayling	2	3 2	......	4 21	5 11	......	6 2	6 52	6 55	6 57	......	7 57	......	8 57
Langston	3	3 6½	..	4 25½	5 15½	..	6 6½	6 56½	6 59½	7 1½	..	8 1½	..	9 1½
HAVANT arr	4	3 10	......	4 29	5 19	......	6 10	7 0	7 3	7 5	......	8 5	......	9 5

These timings WILL APPLY ON SATURDAYS, 22nd June to 14th September, 1957

UP SATURDAYS

		am	am	am	am	am	am	am	am	PM	PM	PM	PM	PM	PM
HAYLING ISLAND .. dep	1	7 2	7 55	8 35	9 45	10 20	10 47	11 20	11 47	12 20	12 47	1 20	1 47	2 20	2 47
North Hayling	2	7 7	8 0	8 40	9 50	......	10 52	......	11 52	......	12 52	......	1 52	......	2 52
Langston	3	7 11½	8 4½	8 44½	9 54½	..	10 56½	..	11 56½	..	12 56½	..	1 56½	..	2 56½
HAVANT arr	4	7 15	8 8	8 48	9 58	10 30	11 0	11 30	12 0	12 30	1 0	1 30	2 0	2 30	3 0

UP SATURDAYS

		PM	PM	PM	PM	PM	PM	PM	PM	PM	PM	PM			
HAYLING ISLAND .. dep	1	3 20	3 47	4 20	4 47	5 20	5 47	6 20	6 49	7 17	7 53	8 52	..	..	..
North Hayling	2	......	3 52	......	4 52	......	5 52	......	6 54	7 22	7 58	8 57	......	......	......
Langston	3	..	3 56½	..	4 56½	..	5 56½	..	6 58½	7 26½	8 2½	9 1½	..	..	..
HAVANT arr	4	3 30	4 0	4 30	5 0	5 30	6 0	6 30	7 2	7 30	8 6	9 5	......	......	......

Hayling Island and Havant A201

These timings WILL APPLY ON SUNDAYS, 23rd June to 15th September, 1957

UP SUNDAYS

			am	am	am	PM	PM	PM	PM	PM	PM	PM	PM	PM	PM
HAYLING ISLAND .. dep	1	..	10 47	11 20	11 47	12 20	12 47	1 20	1 47	2 20	2 47	3 20	3 47	4 20	4 47
North Hayling	2	......	10 52	......	11 52	......	12 52	......	1 52	......	2 52	......	3 52	......	4 52
Langston	3	..	10 56½	..	11 56½	..	12 56½	..	1 56½	..	2 56½	..	3 56½	..	4 56½
HAVANT arr	4	......	11 0	11 30	12 0	12 30	1 0	1 30	2 0	2 30	3 0	3 30	4 0	4 30	5 0

UP SUNDAYS

			PM	PM	PM	PM	PM	PM	PM						
HAYLING ISLAND .. dep	1	..	5 20	5 47	6 20	6 47	7 20	7 47	8 20	..	..	..	..	..	..
North Hayling	2	......	......	5 52	......	6 52	......	7 52	8 25	......	......	......	......	......	......
Langston	3	..	..	5 56½	..	6 56½	..	7 56½	8 29½	..	..	..	..	..	..
HAVANT arr	4	......	5 30	6 0	6 30	7 0	7 30	8 0	8 33	......	......	......	......	......	......

COMMENCES 27th April, 1958

UP SUNDAYS

		am		am		PM	PM		PM	PM		PM	PM		PM
HAYLING ISLAND .. dep	1	10 55	..	11 55	..	12 55	1 55	..	2 55	4 55	..	5 55	6 55	..	7 55
North Hayling	2	11 0	......	12 0	......	1 0	2 0	......	3 0	5 0	......	6 0	7 0	......	8 0
Langston	3	11 4½	..	12 4½	..	1 4½	2 4½	..	3 4½	5 4½	..	6 4½	7 4½	..	8 4½
HAVANT arr	4	11 8	......	12 8	......	1 8	2 8	......	3 8	5 8	......	6 8	7 8	......	8 8

BR (SR) working timetable for the branch (up trains), summer 1957.

On many occasions to obviate light engine working where locomotives were due for changeover, two engines worked a branch train. Restrictions on double heading over Langston bridge meant the second locomotive had to be coupled to the rear of the train. Here 'A1X' class No. 32661 makes for Hayling Island and is approaching East Street overbridge No. 1 between Havant and Langston on 20th July, 1959. The train is formed of non-gangway S1000S and two Maunsell corridor vehicles with 'A1X' class No. 32640 bringing up the rear. Enginemen occasionally contravened this rule and sometimes worked trains double-headed, with the authorities evidently unaware of the illicit practice.   *A. Wright*

'Terrier' No. 32661 departing from Havant with a branch train formed of ex-LSWR brake composite and two BR mark I non-gangway vehicles.   *R.C. Riley*

The tide is out as 'A1X' class 0-6-0T No. 32640, working unusually bunker first, hauls a three-coach down train across Langston Bridge towards Hayling Island. In true branch line malpractice the locomotive displays no headcode. The new timber bridge piers encased in concrete and added by the SR between 1926 and 1931 can be seen to good effect. *Author's Collection*

From the turn of the century until 1925 a siding was provided at North Hayling to cater for the local oyster trade when wagons were loaded with the precious cargo for conveyance to London and Whitstable. The siding could only be served by trains in the up direction so empty wagons were taken through to Hayling Island and then dropped off at the siding when loaded wagons were collected. Here 'A1X' class 0-6-0T No. 32650 approaches North Hayling with an up train on 29th October, 1962, with the site of the siding to the right. The close proximity of the railway to the foreshore and the necessity to carry the line on an embankment to prevent flooding is amply demonstrated in this view. *Ken Paye*

The 11.35 am Havant to Hayling Island train hauled by 'A1X' class 0-6-0T No. 32650 departs from North Hayling in November 1962. The embankment to the left and the railway formation protected the low lying land, to the right of the picture, from flooding. Footpath crossing No 8 bisects the railway between the locomotive and the first coach, a Bulleid corridor brake composite. *Author*

Passengers, including schoolchildren, wend their way off the platform at Hayling Island station, having arrived by the branch train hauled by 'A1X' class 0-6-0T No. 32650. *Author's Collection*

10.19, 11.35 am, 12.35, 1.35, 2.20 SO, 3.35, 4.46, 5.33, 6.20 SX, 6.34 SO, 7.20 SX, 7.34 SO, 8.20 SX and 8.30 pm SO. Up trains departed Hayling Island at 7.02, 7.55, 8.35, 9.45, 10.52, 11.55 am, 12.55, 1.55 SO, 2.57 SO, 2.58 SX, 4.16, 5.06, 5.57, 6.50 SX, 6.52 SO, 7.52 and 8.56 pm. On the last day of public service a special Saturday interval service was operated.

Fares

First, second and third class accommodation was offered on all services from the opening of the line, and the initial fares from Havant to Hayling Island and vice-versa were:

	First Class		Second Class		Third Class	
	s.	d.	s.	d.	s.	d.
Single	1	0	0	9	0	6
Return	1	9	1	0	0	9

For some years the prices remained fairly constant, but were then in fact reduced. Single fares quoted for 1898 from Hayling Island to the branch stations were

	First Class		Second Class		Third Class	
	s.	d.	s.	d.	s.	d.
North Hayling	0	4	0	3	0	2
Langston	0	7	0	4½	0	3½
Havant	0	9	0	6	0	4½

These fares remained in operation until the outbreak of World War I, although by then second class had been abolished.

By 1912 the fares structure from London Victoria or London Bridge was:

	1st single*		3rd single		1st return*		3rd return	
	s.	d.	s.	d.	s.	d.	s.	d.
Havant	11	0	5	6	19	3	11	0
Langston	11	3	5	7	19	5	11	2
North Hayling	11	5	5	8½	19	9	11	5
Hayling Island	11	9	5	10½	20	3	11	9

In the same year season ticket rates between Portsmouth Town and the branch stations were as follows:

	Havant			Langston			North Hayling			Hayling Island		
First class	£	s.	d.	£	s.	d.	£	s.	d	£	s	d.
Annual	10	0	0	11	12	0	13	5	0	13	11	0
Six monthly	5	0	0	5	16	0	6	12	6	6	15	6
Three monthly	2	10	0	2	18	0	3	6	3	3	7	9
Two monthly	2	2	0	2	8	3	2	15	3	2	16	6
One Monthly	1	5	0	1	9	0	1	13	0	1	14	0
Two Weekly	–	–	–	–	–	–	1	4	9	1	5	6
Weekly	–	–	–	–	–	–		16	6		17	0

* Because motor train working was in operation on most services at this period, third class only was available on the branch.

Third Class	£	s.	d.	£	s.	d.	£	s.	d	£	s	d.
Annual	5	10	0	6	7	0	7	16	0	8	0	0
Six monthly	2	15	0	3	3	6	3	18	0	4	0	0
Three monthly	1	7	6	1	11	9	1	19	0	2	0	0
Two monthly	1	3	0	1	6	6	1	12	6	1	13	6
One monthly		13	9		16	0		19	6	1	0	6
Two weekly	–	–	–	–	–	–		14	6		15	0
Weekly	–	–	–	–	–	–		10	0		10	3

Weekend cheap tickets were also available for issue on Friday, Saturday and Sunday for return on Sunday, Monday or Tuesday to or from London at Havant and Hayling Island at a cost of 17s. 6d. first class and 9s. 6d. third class. The facility was not available to Hayling Island on Sundays when the branch was closed.

The fare tariff from London Waterloo to Hayling Island in SR days was:

| | Ordinary returns | | | | Holiday/weekend return | | | | Ordinary single | | | |
| | 1st class | | 3rd class | | 1st class | | 3rd class | | 1st class | | 3rd class | |
Year	s.	d.	s.	d.	s.	d	s	d.	s.	d.	s.	d.
1932	29	8	17	10	20	0	12	0				
1936	18	0	12	0	18	6	9	0	14	10	8	11

| | Cheap monthly returns | | | | Cheap day return | | | | Ordinary single | | | |
Year	s.	d.	s.	d.	s.	d	s	d.	s.	d.	s.	d.
1940	20	9	13	10	15	6	10	4	17	2	10	3

| | Monthly return | | | | Ordinary single | | | |
Year	s.	d.	s.	d.	s.	d.	s.	d.
1942/1944	22	0	14	8	18	2	10	11

During 1947, the last year of Southern Railway operation the fare structure from London Waterloo or Victoria was:

| | 1st single | | | 1st monthly return | | | 3rd single | | | 3rd monthly return | | |
	£	s.	d.	£	s.	d.	£	s.	d	£	s	d.
Havant		19	3	1	3	2		11	9		15	8
Langston		19	8	1	4	2		11	11		16	1
North Hayling	1	0	2	1	4	8		12	2		16	5
Hayling Island	1	0	9	1	5	2		12	5		16	9

In 1955 fares from London Waterloo to the branch stations were:

| | 1st single | | | 1st monthly return | | | 3rd single | | | 3rd monthly return | | |
	£	s.	d.	£	s.	d.	£	s.	d	£	s	d.
Havant		15	11	1	11	10		10	7	1	1	2
Langston		16	0	1	12	0		10	8	1	1	4
North Hayling		16	3	1	12	6		10	10	1	1	8
Hayling Island		16	9	1	13	6		11	2	1	2	4

By 1962 a sample of second class ordinary and mid-week returns fares to Hayling Island were:

From	Ordinary return			Mid-week return*		
	£	s.	d.	£	s.	d.
London (Waterloo)	1	13	0	–	–	–
Birmingham (Snow Hill)	3	14	0	2	16	6
Bradford	5	12	0	4	4	0
Cambridge	2	19	0	2	5	0
Cardiff General	3	8	0	2	11	0
Derby	4	12	0	3	9	0
Edinburgh Waverley	9	4	0	6	18	0
Glasgow Central	9	8	0	7	1	0
Hull	5	12	0	4	4	0
Leeds City	5	10	0	4	2	6
Liverpool	5	12	0	4	4	0
Manchester	5	10	0	4	3	0
Newcastle	6	18	0	5	3	6
Norwich	4	6	0	3	5	0
Nottingham	4	10	0	3	8	0
Preston	5	16	0	4	7	0
Sheffield	5	4	0	3	18	0
Stafford	4	14	0	3	11	0
Swansea High Street	4	9	0	3	7	0
Wolverhampton LL	4	0	0	3	0	0

In the same year the Hayling Island branch was included in South Coast Day Tour Ticket Area 34 which extended from Chichester in the east to Southampton Central in the west and Winchester City in the north at a cost of 9s. 6d. second class. The branch was also included in Holiday Runabout Ticket Area 8 which included the area from Amberley and Littlehampton in the east to Redbridge, Romsey and Winchester in the west at a price of £1 1s. 0d. second class. Travel was available for seven days by all trains but with restrictions between stations east of Cosham at or after 8.30 am on Mondays to Fridays. Both were available during the period 29th April to 27th October.

Guards on the Hayling Island branch trains as well as carrying out their normal duties were responsible for issuing and collecting tickets at North Hayling and the lighting and extinguishing of the oil lamps at Langston and North Hayling.

Goods Traffic

At Langstone wharf, coal and flints for repairing the local roads was offloaded and forwarded by rail. In the 1880s when there were wagons to be picked up or set down at the wharf, the vehicle or vehicles were taken through to South Hayling and then worked back by the 3.10 pm from Hayling with the empty wagons immediately behind the locomotive and in front of the coaching stock. The train would stop just clear of the swing bridge, to allow the guard to uncouple the engine, which would then deliver the empty wagons and or collect the full trucks from the siding and set them back on the train before continuing to Havant. With the silting up of the harbour, however, trade declined and the goods depot closed in 1890. Thereafter the civil engineering department used the siding. The siding on the up side of the line at Langston was used by the ill-fated Marine Transit Company service to and from St Helens on the Isle of Wight using the *Carrier* train ferry vessel. Commencing on 1st September, 1885 and operating initially three times a week, weather permitting,

* Travel out and return on Tuesday, Wednesday or Thursday but not available for return the same week as outward journey (summer months only).

In the latter years mixed trains handled all goods traffic to obviate separate freight workings. On Friday 25th August, 1950 'A1X' class 0-6-0T No. 32661 pulls off Langston viaduct with an up working consisting of two coaches and an array of wagons. The signal in the foreground with Langston Bridge down home signal in the clear position and Langston station up distant at caution denotes that Langston Bridge signal box, just visible to the rear of the train, is switched out. *Author's Collection*

'A1X' class 0-6-0T No. 32661 hauls a mixed train on the approach to Havant on 24th September, 1959. Included in the formation is a Bulleid brake composite and full third, whilst the freight formation consists of five open wagons, one van and two goods brake vans. *E.R. Wethersett*

conveying mainly coal and ballast the service had a chequered existence and ceased operation on 31st March, 1888. A fuller account is related in Chapter Two.

The civil engineering department then used both Langston sidings, until removal of the up side facilities, for the storage of ballast, rails and other equipment and trains serving the sidings were propelled from Havant and restricted to not more than eight 4-wheel or four bogie vehicles loaded or empty with the appropriate goods brake van in the lead. When any movement was made the complete train or a light engine was protected in accordance with the Train Staff and Ticket Regulations.

Oysters were farmed in the waters of Langstone Harbour from 1819 but by 1868 the natural oyster population around the island had been dredged to near extinction by vessels from as far afield as Brightlingsea and Colchester in Essex. Following French practice, the first British oyster beds were successfully resurrected on 900 acres of mudflats near North Hayling and a siding was installed on the up side of the line at 2 miles and 37 chains from Havant, which was used for the loading of oyster traffic, chiefly for conveyance to Whitstable, but other consignments were sent to London. The crop was known locally as Emsworth oysters. If any trucks were required they were taken through to South Hayling and shunted to the rear of an up train so they could be detached and shunted over the points, which formed a trailing connection for up services. After 1907 the guard was responsible for locking and unlocking the points to the siding using the key attached to the Train Staff. He was also responsible for coupling and uncoupling the wagons. The siding was taken out of use by 1925 and the track lifted soon after.

At Hayling as freight traffic increased, the original goods shed was found to be inadequate and was replaced by a larger structure in 1900. Coal, seed potatoes, fertilizers, corn, cement and smalls items for local shops comprised the traffic. Another commodity handled was milk, initially in the familiar 17 gallon churns which were loaded and off-loaded from the brake vans of passenger trains. After World War II a special milk van was retained on the branch to convey the churns. The branch engine ran to the goods yard at Havant to pick up the van of milk before returning to the branch train standing in the bay platform. The van was then worked forward as the leading vehicle on the branch train. After arrival at Hayling Island the engine ran round the stock and on departure of the up working hauled the train clear of No. 6 points before pushing the complete train containing passengers into the goods yard. The van was then detached or fly-shunted before the train continued its journey to Havant. Two loads were conveyed during the summer months, one by an early train and then again in the late afternoon, but only one load was sent in the winter months. Brick traffic was conveyed for some years from Hayling Island, many millions of bricks being dispatched to West Worthing where new housing was being built. In later years Landers, a local builder's merchant at Hayling Island, utilized a former LSWR fruit van SR No. 1615 for the storage of cement and sand.

The relatively small amount of livestock traffic could be handled and horse and carriage traffic loading and unloading facilities were available using the dead-end dock on the up side east end at Havant and the dock at the south end of Hayling Island goods yard.

In World War II shells and other armaments were sometimes conveyed by rail to Langston siding or Hayling Island where the consignments were offloaded and taken by road to the various anti-aircraft gun sites on the island and the coastal area surrounding Langstone Harbour and for military use. The ammunition was usually conveyed in open wagons, sheeted over to conceal the deadly cargo, although two prominent red flashed labels advised 'Shunt With Great Care' and 'Place As Far As Possible From The Engine, Brake Van and Wagons Labelled Inflammable'.

In the late 1950s Shell Mex and BP and Esso were handling oil traffic in Hayling Island goods yard. In the latter years mixed trains were permitted to convey loaded and empty tank wagons across the branch in the event of a special goods train not being available. If conveyed by mixed train, the tank vehicle or vehicles had to be marshalled next inside the rear goods brake van with at least one wagon placed between the tank and vehicles containing passengers or wagons conveying readily combustible material.

In 1963 the goods shed at Hayling Island was used for the storage of wool and cement, and after the *Torrey Canyon* tanker disaster, the local authority stored anti-pollutants. Freight facilities were withdrawn from Hayling Island along with the passenger services on and from 4th November, 1963.

Parcels traffic was always an important feature on the branch and in 1912 the LBSCR was offering a passenger luggage in advance scheme for collection and delivery at Havant and Hayling Island station at a charge of 1s. 0d. per package for rail passengers although the facility was not available for holders of half-day or excursions tickets. For those passengers taking their own package to the station for delivery only from the destination station the price was 6d. per item. SR and BR continued to offer collected luggage (CL), delivered luggage (DL) and passenger luggage in advance (PLA) facilities with increasing prices.

In the halcyon years the following facilities were available for goods and livestock traffic on the branch.

Havant	Loading gauges
	Fixed crane 5 tons capacity (with 18 ft 3 in. height of lift)
	Fixed crane 1 ton capacity
	(with 14 ft 4 in. height of lift - crane in goods shed)
	Goods shed
	Truck weighbridge 20 tons capacity (21 ft in length)
	Loading dock
Langston	Loading gauge
	Fixed crane 1 ton 10 cwt capacity
	(for short period only, later removed)
Hayling Island	Loading gauge
	Fixed crane 1 ton 10 cwt capacity
	(with 14 ft 10 in. height of lift - crane in goods shed)
	Loading dock
	Goods shed
	Lock up for small packages

In order to minimize delay attaching and detaching vehicles in the early years of LBSCR operation coaching stock or wagons requiring detaching were to be positioned at the front of up trains at Hayling Island and at the rear of down trains at Havant.

In LBSCR days the maximum loads of trains on the branch were five bogie coaches, 10 six-wheel coaches or 10 four-wheel coaches. Later the freight train loads book showed that 'A1X' class 0-6-0 tank locomotives were limited to a tail load of 25 standard wagons exclusive of brake van when working from Havant to Hayling Island and return.

Chapter Eight

Locomotives and Rolling Stock

Frederick Furniss used a motley collection of locomotives when he operated the Hayling Railway. The pedigree of No. 1 is unknown but it was thought to have originated as an 0-4-0 saddle tank being rebuilt by Hawthorn & Co. of Leith after 1850. As *Grafton* it arrived on the Isle of Wight in May 1863 and was used by Henry Bond the contractor on the construction of the Isle of Wight Railway, Ryde to Ventnor line until early 1866, by which time both the contractor and the railway company were heavily indebted to the Warrant Finance Co. The locomotive was offered for sale with some of the contractor's plant and described in the *Isle of Wight Times* dated 11th April, 1866 as 'a four wheel locomotive with cylinders 18 inch stroke by Hawthorn and Company Leith'. The locomotive was sold by auction at Wroxall on the same day and purchased by Frederick Furniss for £465. He transferred it to Hayling Island to assist with the construction of the railway, which was completed in July 1867 and thereafter operating the line. The locomotive was painted red and bearing the name *Brighton* worked on the railway until Furniss's contract expired on 31st December, 1871. Whilst working the Hayling service the engine was involved in a near collision with LSWR 2-4-0 tender locomotive *Rufus* and it was only the quick action on the part of Furniss No. 1's driver that averted a major catastrophe. After the LBSCR took over the working of the Hayling Railway in 1872, Furniss sold the locomotive on to I.W. Boulton of Ashton-under-Lyne, a noted dealer in second-hand railway equipment, where it required firebox repairs. Boulton identified the locomotive as *Brighton* and described it as a 0-4-2 box type saddle tank with a haycock firebox dome, having 11 in. x 18 in. cylinders and 3 ft 6 in. diameter wheels. The date of conversion from 0-4-0 to 0-4-2 wheel arrangement is not known. It was hired out on several occasions before being sold in 1875 or 1876 to Brunner, Mond & Co. for use at their Northwich, Cheshire chemical works where it was finally scrapped.

The second engine used by Furniss was an 0-4-2 saddle tank locomotive built by George England & Co. at Hatcham Ironworks, Peckham, London. Numbered 2 by Furniss, this engine was originally built as an 0-4-0 tank engine with 9½ in. x 13 in. cylinders, 2 ft 10 in. diameter driving wheels. The locomotive certainly looked strange when Furniss added 3 feet diameter trailing wheels during the conversion of the wheel arrangement to provide stability on Hayling services. About 1871 No. 2 went to Boulton's Yard, where it was named *Portsmouth*.

A third locomotive operated on the Hayling Railway services was an A. Hughes & Co. 0-4-0 saddle tank with 3 ft 0 in. wheels and 10 in. x 15 in. cylinders, which had formerly worked on the Portsmouth drainage contract. The engine was totally underpowered and Furniss replaced it by hiring LBSCR No. 115, both on the drainage contract and for working the Hayling branch.

The Hayling passenger service was then largely worked by a 2-4-0 tender locomotive, rebuilt by Boulton to a 2-4-0 saddle tank engine named *Wootton*, to replace Furniss Nos. 1 and 2. It was thought to have been built by Hawthorn and had 15 in. x 20 in. cylinders and 5 ft 0 in., later 4 ft 0 in., driving wheels, and in this guise was considered to be more suitable for passenger traffic. After being returned to Boulton in 1872 it became a pit winding engine in Scotland.

Furniss relinquished working the Hayling Railway on 31st December, 1871, and from adoption the following day the LBSCR was undecided as to which type of

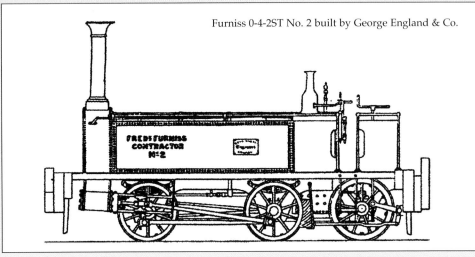

Furniss 0-4-2ST No. 2 built by George England & Co.

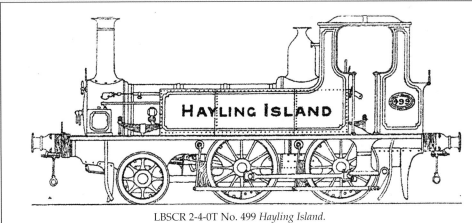

LBSCR 2-4-0T No. 499 *Hayling Island*.

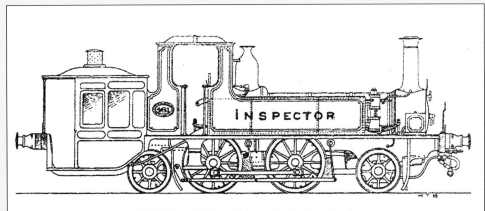

LBSCR 2-4-0T No. 461 formerly *Hayling Island*
as converted to an inspection vehicle and named *Inspector*.

locomotive to use on the branch, for the severe weight limitation imposed by Langston bridge somewhat restricted the choice of motive power available. Various ageing machines were utilized until 1874, when a Sharp, Stewart-built 2-4-0 tank locomotive (Works No. 1924) arrived to work the services. Originally delivered on 30th September, 1869, the locomotive, numbered 96, worked the Kensington shuttle service for three years, when it was rebuilt, named *Kemptown* and sent to Brighton shed to work the Kemp Town line. In 1874 it was displaced by a 'Terrier' tank engine and lost its name which was acquired by 'Terrier' tank locomotive No. 64. The 2-4-0 was subsequently again renumbered to 115 and named *Hayling Island* whence it was sent to Portsmouth shed for the Hayling line. So suitable was the engine for the branch that it continued to work the services regularly for the next 15 years until 1889. *Hayling Island* was successively renumbered 359 in June 1877 and 499 in January 1886. The Westinghouse brake had been added and a new firebox and brass tubes were fitted in December 1888. At the close of 1889 William Stroudley, the LBSCR locomotive superintendent, withdrew the engine from traffic for rebuilding with a small inspection saloon behind the bunker, so that it could be used for inspecting the line. It emerged from Brighton works in January 1890 suitably modified, but because of the death of Stroudley, it was infrequently used by the engineer's department and was withdrawn for scrapping in March 1898 and cut up in January 1899.

The principal dimensions of *Hayling Island* were:

Motion		Stephenson with slide valve
Cylinders		10 in. x 16 in.
Leading wheels		2 ft 9 in.
Coupled wheels		4 ft 0 in.
Wheelbase		11 ft 0 in.
Boiler	*diameter*	2 ft 10 in.
	length	8 ft 6 in.
Boiler pressure		120 psi
Heating surface	*tubes*	75 x 1⅝ in. – 278.47 sq. ft
	firebox	33.75 sq. ft
	total	312.22 sq. ft
Firebox		2 ft 8 in.
Grate area		7.25 sq. ft
Water capacity		410 gallons
Weight in working order		19 tons 8 cwt
Max axle loading		7 tons 0 cwt

From May 1878 *Hayling Island* was joined by another Sharp, Stewart 2-4-0 tank engine named *Fratton*. Four locomotives were originally built in 1872 to an order placed by the Tunis & Goletta Railway (Sharp, Stewart Works Nos. 2241/2/3/4) but when ready only two were sent, and of the remaining engines No. 2241 became Jersey Railway *North Western*, which was subsequently transferred to the Jersey Eastern Railway, whilst Stroudley purchased No. 2242 for £1,600 in 1873. Painted in a bright grass green livery with large dome in polished brass casing it was initially numbered 53 by the LBSCR, and worked on the West London Extension Railway until it was renumbered 270, named *Bishopstone* and sent to Newhaven for light shunting duties. A further renumbering took place in 1878, when as No. 357 and renamed *Fratton* it shared duties on the Hayling Island branch. In April 1886 it was withdrawn from the line and sent to Brighton works for the fitting of new cylinders and small leading wheels before renumbering yet again to No. 497. On emerging

From May 1878 Sharp, Stewart 2-4-0T *Fratton* jointly worked the branch with *Hayling Island*. It was initially numbered 53 by the LBSCR and then 270 named *Bishopstone* and sent for light shunting duties at Newhaven. A further renumbering took place in 1878 when as No. 357 she was renamed *Fratton* and shared duties on the Hayling Island line. In April 1886 it was withdrawn from the line but after modification and yet further renumbering to 497 she served some months as Brighton works pilot engine before returning to the Hampshire branch. It was withdrawn from traffic in September 1890.   *Author's Collection*

LBSCR 0-4-2ST No. 358 *Bognor* which, as No. 496, served on the Hayling line between 1890 and 1895.

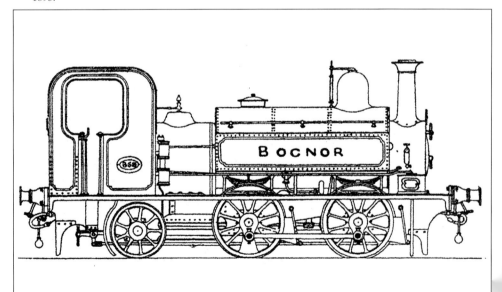

from the works it was not immediately returned to the Hayling Island branch and served some months as Brighton works pilot engine before migrating back to Hampshire. Withdrawal from traffic for scrapping took place in September 1890 and the locomotive was sold to George Cohen & Sons in October 1890 for £164.

The leading dimensions of *Fratton* were:

Motion		Stephenson with slide valves
Cylinders		12 in. x 17 in.
Leading wheels		2 ft 9 in.
Coupled wheels		4 ft 0 in.
Wheelbase		12 ft 5 in.
Boiler	*diameter*	3 ft 3 in.
	length	9 ft 0 in.
Firebox length		3 ft 7 in.
Grate area		7.50 sq. ft
Boiler pressure		140 psi
Heating surface	*tubes*	523.0 sq. ft
	firebox	47.0 sq. ft
	total	570.0 sq. ft
Water capacity		400 gallons

Between 1890 and 1895 Kitson 0-4-2 saddle tank locomotive No. 496 *Bognor* was utilized on Hayling Island services. The engine, which had originally been purchased for £1,140 (Works No. 1553), was delivered to the LBSCR on 17th May, 1869 and numbered 76. Initially the locomotive was used in the London area but by early 1870 was transferred to Littlehampton. The engine was rebuilt by Stroudley in 1872 with sides to the cab, copper-capped chimney and taller dome cover. It was then named *Bognor* and was sent to that town to work the shuttle service to Barnham Junction. However, after a few months the engine returned to Littlehampton shed for use on the Arundel trains. In June 1877 the engine was renumbered 358 and in 1882 received new cylinders and a new firebox. In August 1886 the locomotive was renumbered yet again to 496 and by 1890 was working the Hayling Island branch, although for a short period in 1891 it was working from Eastbourne. No 496 returned to service on the Hayling line until finally withdrawn from traffic in April 1895.

The principal dimensions of No 496 *Bognor* as rebuilt and working on the Hayling Island branch were:

Motion		Stephenson with slide valves
Cylinders		12 in. x 18 in.
Coupled wheels		4 ft 0 in.
Trailing wheels		3 ft 0 in.
Wheelbase		12 ft 2 in.
Boiler	*diameter*	3 ft 0 in.
	length	9 ft 7 in.
Firebox length		3 ft 6 in.
Boiler pressure		140 psi
Grate area		9.0 sq ft
Heating surface	*tubes*	110 x 1¾ ins – 452.0 sq. ft
	firebox	52.0 sq. ft
	total	504.0 sq. ft
Weight in working order		17 tons 2 cwt
Water capacity		496 gallons
Max axle loading		6 tons 11 cwt

Between 1890 and 1895 Kitson 0-4-2ST No. 496 *Bognor* was utilized on Hayling services. It had been delivered to the LBSCR in May 1869 and initially numbered 76 worked in the London area. By 1870 it was transferred to Littlehampton but was rebuilt in 1872 and named *Bognor* sent to work the shuttle services from that town to Barnham Junction. Further renumbering to 358 was made in 1877 and new cylinders and firebox were fitted in 1882. In 1886 it was renumbered to 496 and, except for a short sojourn at Eastbourne, worked the Hayling services until withdrawn in April 1895.   *Author's Collection*

Kitson 0-4-2ST LBSCR No. 496 *Bognor* as modified by Stroudley for service on the Bognor branch and ultimately on Havant to Hayling Island services between 1890 and 1895.
                                                                    Author's Collection

On the withdrawal of *Fratton* from the Hayling line a substitute locomotive had to be found, initially as a standby to No. 499 *Hayling Island* and then for No. 496 *Bognor*. At this period some of the Stroudley 'A' later 'A1' class 0-6-0 tank locomotives nicknamed 'Rooters' or more popularly 'Terriers' and originally introduced in 1872, were being rendered surplus to original requirements and it was soon found that their light axle loading and adequate tractive effort were ideal for the line. Gradually members of the class were cascaded to the branch and from 1895 when the 0-4-2 saddle tank locomotive was withdrawn from traffic, the 0-6-0 tank engines reigned supreme until the closure of the line in November 1963, being the only permitted engines on the branch in later LBSCR, SR and BR days.

By 1890 Portsmouth shed was allocated four of the 'A1' class to work the Hayling and Southsea branches, No. 43 *Gipsyhill*, No. 48 *Leadenhall*, No. 71 *Wapping* and No. 78 *Knowle*, with one usually sub-shedded at South Hayling. In the first years of operation No. 48 *Leadenhall* was regularly working the line, covered during times of maintenance or shopping by No. 78 *Knowle*. A few years later locomotives due for works repairs or near to scrapping worked out their last days between Havant and Hayling and No. 663 *Kemptown* went for scrapping in 1903 after handling the branch services for some months prior to withdrawal. Around this time the locomotives lost their names and to make way for more modern locomotives the 'Terriers' were renumbered generally by having 600 added to their former LBSCR numbers. Many were then reboilered and became class 'A1X'.

In January 1907 motor-train working was established between Havant and Hayling Island, and to cope with the service Nos. 643 and 673 were fitted with the necessary equipment. In 1911 the allocation to Fratton shed, which had replaced Portsmouth shed, was Nos. 673, 679 and 680. By March 1912 Nos. 650 and 679 had joined Nos. 643, whilst No. 673 was transferred away elsewhere on the LBSCR system. During World War I No. 663 became the regular Hayling branch engine but soon after hostilities it was found the push-pull system was not entirely satisfactory. Motor train working was replaced by manual haulage with the engine running-round the train at each terminal. The 'Balloon' single class carriage used on the motor trains was unpopular as it had insufficient accommodation for the ever-increasing traffic in the summer months, whilst the running of mixed trains found the push-pull method of operation an inconvenience.

After Grouping the Southern Railway found no cause for complaint with the class and continued using the 'Terriers' on the branch services. Fratton shed and the Hayling Island branch was transferred to the London Western District, thus severing the connections with the former Brighton section. Gradually the motor-train gear was removed from the locomotives and vacuum ejectors fitted, to allow the engines to work with vacuum-braked stock. Former LBSCR locomotives were also given a prefix 'B' to denote their former ownership but were later renumbered by having 2000 added to the existing numbers. By 1925 Fratton shed was allocating Nos. B635, B655 and B662 to the Hayling services and just over a decade later an even larger allocation of locomotives was available to handle the branch traffic. Nos. 2635, 2655, 2659, 2661 and 2662 were joined in July 1937 by No. 2678, which had returned from exile on the Isle of Wight where it was No. 14 *Bembridge*. During World War II some of Fratton's 'Terriers' were drafted away from the coastal area to other SR depots, in case of invasion, so that by 1942 Nos. 2635 and 2662 were the regular branch engines, with Nos. 2644 and 2655 as shed pilot and spare engine.

After nationalization in January 1948 British Railways, Southern Region could find no adequate motive power replacements for these minute tank locomotives and

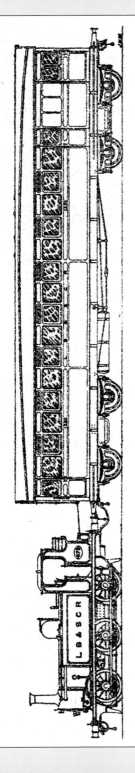

LBSCR 'A1' class 0-6-0T No. 673 and balloon brake/third driving trailer used on the push-pull services on the branch.

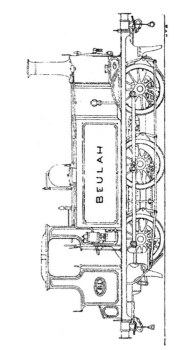

LBSCR 'A1' class 0-6-0T No. 81 *Beulah*, which worked the Hayling line during its career.

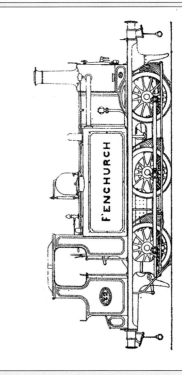

LBSCR 'A1' class 0-6-0T No. 72 *Fenchurch*, which as BR No. 32636 worked the last train across the Hayling Island branch on 3rd November, 1963.

their continuing work on the line was assured. The previous year No. 2640 had arrived at Fratton to take its turn on the Hayling Island branch duties after service on the Isle of Wight, where it had been No. 11 *Newport*. This locomotive was the famed LBSCR No. 40 *Brighton*, which had gained a gold medal award for Stroudley at the Paris Exhibition in 1878. By 1949 the class was being repainted in BR lined black livery and 30000 was added to the running number. In the summer of that year Fratton shed had command of Nos. 32646, 2655, 32659, 2661, 32662 and 32677 of which two were utilized on the Hayling branch on Saturdays and one each weekday. The first and last of these, Nos. 32646 and 32677, had recently returned from exile on the Isle of Wight where they had been Nos. 8 *Freshwater* and 13 *Carisbrooke* respectively. The former was well travelled, having been LBSCR No. 46 *Newington* before sale to the LSWR in 1903 for work on the Lyme Regis branch when it became No. 734. Ten years later it was sold to the Freshwater, Yarmouth & Newport Railway becoming No. 2 in that company's fleet. In August 1923 the SR acquired the undertaking and it became No. W2 and later W8 and carrying the name *Freshwater*.

Gradually the work allocated to the 'Terrier' tank locomotives diminished and in the last decade of service on British Railways duties were divided between the Newhaven Harbour lines and the Hayling Island branch. When Fratton depot officially closed on 2nd November, 1959, the allocation of the 'A1X' class Nos. 32636, 32640, 32646, 32650, 32661 and 32678 was transferred to Eastleigh for maintenance, although the engine allocated to work the Hayling branch continued to be stabled overnight at Fratton.

With the last duties at Newhaven replaced by diesel shunting locomotives, the Hayling Island branch became the last outpost for the activities of the 'A1X' class 'Terriers'. Enthusiasts journeyed miles in the last few months of service to ride behind the veteran machines. Unfortunately their mechanical condition deteriorated and lack of readily available spares, unavailability of suitable replacements, despite the lifting of the prohibition on the former South Eastern & Chatham Railway 'P' class 0-6-0 tank locomotives, and the condition of Langston bridge were all contributing factors to the proposal for the withdrawal of all services between Havant and Hayling Island. 'P' class locomotive No. 31325, nominally allocated to Brighton shed, but temporarily based at Eastleigh depot and at the time sub-shedded at Winchester deputizing for a 'B4' class 0-4-0 tank engine on shunting duties, was sent for evaluation trials on the Hayling Island line and worked the branch services on 12th June, 1957. The engine was considered not to have the power of the 'A1X' engines and was soon back at Winchester.

On the last day of public working Saturday 2nd November, 1963, Nos. 32650, 32662 and 32670 were in charge of the augmented service, whilst for the final run across the branch on Sunday 3rd November the LCGB's 'Hayling Farewell' Railtour train Nos. 32636 and 32670 were provided, the former at the Hayling end of the train and the latter at the Havant end. No. 32636 was specifically chosen for the tour being, at that time, the oldest working steam engine in service with British Railways.

In the latter years of working the line the 'Terrier' tank engines were fitted with small spark arresters over their chimneys, to obviate fire damage to farm crops and gardens adjacent to the line from showers of sparks. The last remaining locomotives of the class were withdrawn in November 1963 but most survived the cutters' torch and were purchased by railway preservation societies. Locomotives known to have been associated with the Hayling Island branch included:

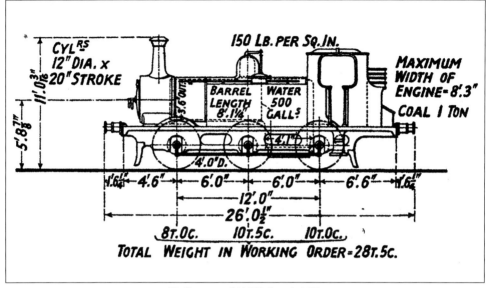

SR diagram of 'A1X' class 0-6-0T.

SR diagram of 'P' class 0-6-0T.

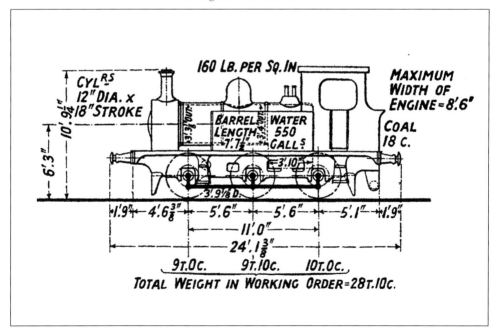

LBSC 1st No.	Name	LBSC 2nd No.	SR 1st No.	SR 2nd No.	BR No.	Date rebuilt to 'A1X'	Withdrawn	Notes
35	Morden	635	B635	2635	32635	04.1922	03.1963	
				377s	DS377			
40	Brighton		W11	2640	32640	08.1918	09.1963	1
43	Gipsyhill	643*	–	–	5	09.1919	12.1925	2
44	Fulham	644	B644	2644	32644	11.1912	04.1951	
46	Newington	646	W2	W8	32646	12.1932	11.1963	3
48	Leadenhall	648	–	–	–		08.1901	
50	Whitechapel	650	W9/515s	DS515	32650	05.1920	11.1963	4
53	Ashstead	653	B653	–	–	05.1912	02.1937	5
55	Stepney	655	B655	2655	32655	12.1912	05.1960	12
59	Cheam	659	B659	2659	32659	12.1921	06.1963	
					DS681			
61	Sutton	661	B661	2661	32661	12.1912	04.1963	
62	Martello	662	B662	2662	32662	12.1912	11.1963	
63	Preston	663	–	–	–	12.1913	03.1925	
64	Kemptown	664	–	–	–		01.1903	
70	Poplar	–	–	–	32670	12.1943	11.1963	6
71	Wapping	671	–	–	–		01.1905	7
72	Fenchurch	–	B636	2636	32636	12.1913	11.1963	8
73	Deptford	673*	–	–	–	12.1912	04.1919	9
77	Wonersh	677	W3	W13	32677	11.1911	09.1959	
78	Knowle	678	W4	W14	32678	11.1911	10.1963	10
					2678			
79	Minories	679*	–	–	–	12.1912	01.1918	11
80	Bookham	680*	–	–	–	12.1925	12.1925	
81	Beulah	681	–	–	–		01.1918	13

1. Sold to Isle of Wight Central Railway December 1901 became their No 11; renumbered W11 by SR in April 1924 and named *Newport* in 1930; returned to mainland to become 2640 in 1947.
2. Sold to Weston Clevedon & Portishead Railway in December 1925 becoming their No 2 *Portishead*, became Great Western Railway No. 5 in 1940 and passed to BR as No. 5 before withdrawal in 1950; scrapped 1954.
3. Sold in 1903 to LSWR, who numbered it 734; sold on in 1913 to the Freshwater, Yarmouth and Newport Railway. On entering SR stock renumbered W2 in 1924 and named *Freshwater* in 1928; renumbered W8 in 1932 and returned to the mainland in 1948 to become 32646.
4. Transferred to the Isle of Wight in 1930 as W9 *Fishbourne*; returned to mainland 1936 and sent to Lancing carriage works as 515s in 1937; renumbered DS 515 in 1948 before becoming 32650 in 1953.
5. Sold to Weston, Clevedon & Portishead Railway in February 1937 becoming that railway's No. 4, taken over by GWR 1940 and withdrawn in 1948.
6. Sold in 1901 to the Rother Valley Railway, later Kent & East Sussex Railway becoming No. 3 *Bodiam*. Taken over by BR in 1948 and renumbered 32670.
7. Sold 1901 to Rother Valley Railway later Kent & East Sussex Railway becoming No. 5 *Rolvenden*; cannibalized in 1933 to keep No. 3 in service and cut up in 1938.
8. Sold 1898 to Newhaven Harbour Co.; harbour company taken over by the SR in 1925 and locomotive renumbered B636 in 1927, then 2636.
9. Loaned to Longmoor Military Railway 1916; sold to Edge Hill Light Railway in April 1919 as No. 1. After the line closed in 1925 the locomotive rusted away until the remains were cut up in 1946.
10. Sent to Isle of Wight in 1929 as W4 *Bembridge* before being renumbered W14 in 1932; returned to the mainland in 1936 as No. 2678 and used on the Kent and East Sussex line from 1941 to 1949.
11. Sold to Admiralty in January 1918 for use in Chatham Dockyard and scrapped in 1933.
12. Withdrawn 1925 reinstated 1927.
13. Sold January 1918 to the Government for use on light military railways, resold to the Shropshire & Montgomeryshire Light Railway, became No. 3 *Hecate*, sold for scrap October 1934.

* Fitted with motor train equipment.

View of the cab of 'A1X' class 0-6-0T No. 32650 on 29th October, 1963. *R. Powell*

The principal dimensions of the 'A' later 'A1' and 'A1X' locomotives were:

	'A1' 'Terrier' original dimensions	'A1X' 'Terrier' rebuilt dimensions
Cylinders	13 in. x 20 in.	12 in. x 20 in. (Nos. 32635/44/50/55/59/61/62/77) 13 in. x 20 in. (No. 32646) 14 in. x 20 in. (Nos. 32636/40/70/78)
Coupled wheels	3 ft 11½ in.	4 ft 0 in.
Wheelbase	12 ft 0 in.	12 ft 0 in.
Boiler		
diameter	3 ft 6 in.	3 ft 6 in.
length	7 ft 10 in.	8 ft 1¼ in.
Boiler pressure	140 psi	150 psi
Heating surface		
tubes (125 x 1¾ in.)	473.0 sq. ft	433.2 sq. ft*
firebox	55.0 sq. ft	55.6 sq. ft
total	528.0 sq. ft	488.8 sq. ft
Firebox	4 ft 1 in.	4 ft 1 in.
Grate area	10.3 sq. ft	10.0 sq. ft
Tank capacity	500 gallons	500 gallons
Bunker capacity	10 cwt	10cwt/1 ton
Max. axle loading	8 tons 4 cwt	10 tons 5 cwt
Weight in working order	26 tons 17 cwt	28 tons 5 cwt

* Recorded in BR diagram book as tubes 119 x 1¾ in.

Despite their considerable age the 'Terrier' tank locomotives were capable of lively performances in the final years on the Hayling Island branch. Typical examples on the non-stop summer Saturday services included No. 32650 hauling four coaches and a bogie van passing Langston in 3 minutes 17 seconds at 49 mph, and after slowing for the swing bridge cleared North Hayling in 5 minutes 28 seconds, before arriving at Hayling Island in an overall time of 9 minutes 5 seconds for the journey, with a top speed of 53 mph between North Hayling and the terminus. The return run was accomplished in 10 minutes 2 seconds with a top speed of 48 mph. Sister locomotive No. 32640 with the same tail load passed Langston in 3 minutes 22 seconds, North Hayling 5 minutes 56 seconds with 9 minutes 58 seconds to the terminus at a top speed of 48 mph. No. 32640 returned to Havant in 10 minutes 6 seconds achieving 52 mph approaching North Hayling.

Although the 'Terrier' tank locomotives reigned supreme on the Hayling Island branch, at Havant 'N' and 'U' class 2-6-0, 'Q' and 'Q1' class 0-6-0 and 'T9' class 4-4-0 tender locomotives were permitted between the station and home the from-Hayling signal for the purpose of attaching vehicles to trains working through to Cosham and beyond. The Havant goods yard pilot locomotive could also propel wagons to Langston siding and work back to the junction in the event of the non-availability of a 'Terrier' tank locomotive.

The headcode carried by the locomotive operating the branch in LBSCR, SR and BR days was one white circular disc during daylight and one white light during the hours of darkness, fog or falling snow, on the lamp bracket over the right-hand buffer facing

'A1X' class 0-6-0T No. 32640 has just arrived at Hayling Island with the two-coach 12.35 pm train from Havant on 12th May, 1956 as two schoolboys take an interest in the locomotive as they leave the platform. The locomotive still carries the tapering style of chimney fitted during her service on the Isle of Wight. *R. Buckley*

Looking north under the remains of the canopy at Hayling Island with LBSCR non-gangway bogie stock forming the branch train to the right and stabled in the bay platform to the left. *Author's Collection*

forward from the driver's cab. In LBSCR days if a special train travelled over the branch the locomotive carried a white disc over the right buffer and a white disc with a cross at the chimney. In addition, if any train carried the Train Staff Ticket and not the Train Staff, a white disc was carried over both right- and left-hand buffers.

When the Hayling Railway first opened between Havant and Langston Quay the locomotive working the line was stabled in a shed on the down side of the railway mid-way between the half and three-quarter mile posts, close to where the later A27 road crossed the railway. A water tank was also provided alongside the structure. After completion of the extension to South Hayling this shed was closed and the siding removed. A shed was then provided at the back of South Hayling station platform in 1874, complete with coal stage and water tank and a locomotive was outbased from Portsmouth shed to work the branch. The shed building had originally been at Petworth before transfer to South Hayling. This arrangement lasted until 1894 after which the branch engine was worked out and back from Portsmouth, later replaced by Fratton shed (BR shed code 71D, later 70F). The shed at South Hayling was demolished a few years later. The water supply was abolished and the coal stage transferred to a point between the run-round loop and the goods shed road in 1902. When Fratton shed closed in 1959 the branch locomotives were allocated to Eastleigh (BR code 71A) where they received repairs and maintenance but continued to be outbased at Fratton as it was retained as a signing-on point for staff.

Initially only one set of men was working the 12 hour shift from South Hayling shed, signing on at 7.55 am until going off duty at 7.55 pm. Alf Upton, a Fratton driver, came over weekly to give the Hayling driver a half-day off. Later two sets of footplatemen were stationed at South Hayling but after 1894, when the shed closed, the locomotives and men came from Portsmouth and later Fratton shed working light engine from Fratton to Hayling Island in the morning and returning after the last Hayling Island branch train in the evening. After 1896 the engine worked the 6.55 am passenger train from Portsmouth through to Hayling Island to return with the 7.55 am first up branch service. After the passage of the last up branch train in the evening the engine returned with the empty stock from Havant to Fratton following the 6.25 pm ex-Brighton to Portsmouth train, which departed Havant at 8.04 pm. Later the engine worked empty coaching stock from Fratton to Havant in the morning and returned with the stock after the last branch train at night. The new workings required two sets of men, with crews changing over at Havant at 2.00 pm ready to take the 2.05 pm train to Hayling Island. The back shift men were signed on to perform shunting duties at Fratton with the yard pilot engine before travelling passenger to Havant to relieve the early turn men. At that time drivers were paid 7s. 0d. per day and firemen 3s. 6d. Fratton footplate staff working the branch in the latter years included drivers Percy Osborne, Weekes, Hearn, Chick, Fellowes who retired in September 1963, D. Sessions, G. McAskill and Beard and firemen Phillips, Lee and Bradbury.

After the closure of the shed at South Hayling in 1894, water for replenishing locomotives was obtained from a small water crane located by the buffer stops at Havant station bay platform. Hand coaling of the engine was executed at Hayling Island from a small coal stage located adjacent to the run-round loop. Hand coaling was also performed from a coal stage located alongside Leggett's siding at Havant when the timetable required the turn-over engine to wait at the junction for its next turn of duty. The coal was offloaded from a wagon standing on the siding on to the coal stage and then from coal stage to locomotive bunker by a shed labourer or cleaner from Fratton.

Hand coaling of 'A1X' class No. 32650 at Hayling Island on 29th October, 1962. The wagons, including an ex-private owner eight plank open, stand on the adjacent dock road.   *Ken Paye*

The headshunt at the end of the bay platform road at Havant on 29th October, 1962 as the fireman prepares to replenish No. 32650 with water and the driver contacts the signal box to tell the signalman to alter the points to allow the locomotive to run-round the train.   *Ken Paye*

In SR days Fratton depot duty numbers were 360 to 376 inclusive and the duty numbers carried by the 'Terrier' tanks working the branch included at various times Nos. 374, 375 and 376, although on summer Saturdays a rearrangement of duties found No. 222 working the line.

Steam breakdown cranes were prohibited from working over the Hayling Island branch and in the event of a major breakdown or derailment, tool vans from Portsmouth, later Fratton motive power depot, latterly Nos. DS3191, DS3192 and DS232, were obtained and propelled to the site of the incident. In LBSCR days Havant East signal box was provided with four single rerailing ramps whilst two hand screw jacks and two traversing jacks were held in the staff room. Three hand screw jacks were also held in the carriage examiner's lobby. Hayling Island had one traversing jack held in the goods shed. In SR days Havant station was provided with eight single ramps, two point ramps, two hand screw jacks, two traversing jacks and a tool box to cover emergencies, whilst Hayling Island station had one traversing jack.

Coaching Stock

The initial service operated by Furniss made use of four-wheel, three-compartment first class, four-compartment second and third class coaches, measuring 19 ft 6 in. over headstocks and with 10 ft 6 in. wheelbase dating from 1859, hired from the LSWR. An LSWR 19 ft passenger luggage and brake van with 10 ft 0 in. wheelbase would have completed the formation. These were returned when the LBSCR assumed responsibility in 1872. In the early years the four-wheel stock comprised three-compartment composites, four-compartment thirds and full brakes of the pre-Stroudley era. Then from the 1880s, the regular branch train was formed of Stroudley four-wheel stock, including full brake, full third, composite and brake third. The full brake at this period was often a 20 ft-long passenger luggage van to LBSCR diagram 47. The train was strengthened in summer with two more full thirds and an extra composite. These vehicles were built between 1872 and 1892 to a standard length of 26 ft and a width of 8 ft, the bodies were mahogany with teak framing and the wooden underframes were teak. Many Stroudley vehicles were withdrawn between 1899 and 1910 but a number survived until 1923 and in 1916 set No. 20 was allocated to the branch service which was composed of four-wheel brake third No. 1070 dating from 1881, composite No. 174 dating from 1878 and brake third No. 104 dating from 1890.

At the turn of the century the LBSCR management were concerned their system was being operated at a loss brought about by the increasing cost of locomotive coal and dwindling receipts, the latter especially around South London, Brighton and Portsmouth where the introduction of electric tramways had brought direct competition to the railway. Some branch lines also experienced reduced receipts and auto-train working was introduced from 1905 on certain routes initially with two petrol-electric cars and then two self-contained steam railmotors. These were not wholly satisfactory and so the decision was made to provide separate auto-train trailer coaches pulled and pushed by the 'A1' class 'Terrier' 0-6-0 tank locomotives and later by the 'D1' class 0-4-2 tank engines. Thus in January 1907 motor train working was established on the Hayling Island branch to reduce operating costs using 'Balloon' stock dating from 1905 and 1906 with some later additions added in 1907. It is uncertain which individual vehicles were used on the branch services but they were all driving trailer thirds, which were similar in appearance. LBSCR Nos.

1326 and 1327 (later SR Nos. 3829 and 3830) and dating from 1905 were to LBSCR diagram 179 (later SR diagram 190), seated 52 passengers and had a tare weight of 24 tons 5 cwt whilst LBSCR Nos. 1328 to 1333, SR Nos. 3831 to 3836 built in 1906 to LBSCR diagram 180 (later SR diagram 191) seated 60 and weighed 24 tons 5 cwt if gas lit and 25 tons if lit by electricity. The third variant dating from 1907 was LBSCR Nos. 1334 to 1342 later SR Nos. 3837 to 3845, to LBSCR diagram 181 (later SR diagram 192) which seated 60 third class passengers. The three types had a uniform dimension but differed internally and when new the livery was umber with white upper panels, the moulding being umber lined out in yellow but at the first repaint the vehicles became all-over brown.

Length over buffers	57 ft 11 in.
Length over body	54 ft 0 in.
Width over body	8 ft 10 in.
Width over stepboards	9 ft 6 in.
Height	12 ft 11 in.
Bogie centres	37 ft 0 in.

Originally the coaches had mechanical linkage control with the driver operating the regulator and brakes from the driver's compartment with the fireman remaining on the locomotive. The mechanical control was unsatisfactory and was replaced by air pressure control after 1909, although this involved the coupling of four hoses; the main train pipe, back pressure pipe, main storage pipe and regulator pipe. In all four 'Terrier' tank locomotives equipped with the necessary gear are known to have been allocated to auto-train working on the branch. The 'Balloon' coach had a driver's compartment containing levers for operating the regulator and brake which obviated the necessity for detaching the engine at terminal stations. A whistle operated by compressed air was also provided at the rear end of the coach. Unfortunately the accommodation of the single coach was overwhelmed at busy periods, especially in the summer months and normal coaches were substituted. The coach was also an operational inconvenience with mixed train working when wagons required attaching or detaching to or from the formation, and shortly after the outbreak of World War I auto-train working ceased between Havant and Hayling Island in 1916.

After Grouping the SR introduced low-roofed former LSWR non-corridor bogie coaches to the branch including a two-car set formed of a 42 ft-long brake third with 7 ft bogies and 27 ft 9 in. bogie centres and a 45 ft brake composite, the latter with 8 ft bogies and 28 ft 9 in. bogie centres. These were followed by arc-roofed short-bodied non-corridor ex-LSWR coaches of the same dimensions, save the brake third had 8 ft bogies with 28 ft 3 in. bogie centres, although in July 1931 'Terrier' No. 655 was noted taking a special train of 10 LSWR six-wheel coaches on the branch. These were interspersed with ex-LBSCR stock and in 1936 ex-LBSCR motor train set No. 793 was allocated to the branch workings but not worked in the push-pull mode. Unlike former years this was not 'Balloon' stock. This set was still in use in 1937 and 1939 and was formed of the following vehicles: driving trailer brake third to LBSCR diagram 182 (SR diagram 189), former LBSCR No. 1343 (later SR No. 3825) with driving compartment. The vehicle dating from December 1911 seated 56 third class passengers and weighed 25 tons. This was coupled to trailer composite LBSCR diagram 110 (later SR diagram 346), former LBSCR No. 640 (later SR No. 6201) also dating from December 1911, which seated 19 first and 48 third class passengers and had a tare weight of 23 tons. Both coaches had a body length of 54 ft 0 in., 57 ft 7 in. length over buffers and width of 8 ft. This set was transferred to the Isle of Wight in May 1947 and worked the Merstone to Ventnor West branch until the line closed in September 1952, after which no useful work could be found and the pair were withdrawn from traffic in May 1954. On the Isle of Wight the duo became set 505 with the driving trailer third brake renumbered 4167 and the composite trailer No. 6366.

Another motor-train set used on the Hayling Island line for a short time in 1939 was set 727 formed of trailer brake third to LBSCR diagram 183 (later SR diagram 188), LBSCR No. 1350 dating from December 1912 (and later SR No. 3824) weighing 25 tons and seating 64 third class passengers together with trailing composite to LBSCR diagram 114 (and SR diagram 349), seating 19 first and 48 third class passengers and weighing 24 tons. Both vehicles were 57 ft 7 in. over buffers, with 54 ft 0 in. body and width of 8 ft. This set was withdrawn from service in January 1959. Later coach sets were replaced by loose stock and in 1944 former LSWR third No. 616 and brake composite No. 6510 were working the branch.

British Railways initially used former LSWR and LBSCR stock alongside SR coaches and in 1950 the branch allocation was ex-LSWR composite brakes Nos. 6518 and 6541 with ex-LSWR third class Nos. 253 and 640, usually with a single vehicle or a pair stabled at Hayling Island. In 1952 ex-LSWR composite brake Nos. 6484 and 6518 were allocated for winter services either working singly or as a pair. By 1955 ex-LSWR brake/third No. 2650, together with composite No. 4753 and brake composite No. 6529 were allocated to the Hayling Island services. In May 1957 the first of a number of new BR-built compartment seconds arrived and several of the batch allocated to the Southern Region, Nos. 46280 to 46298, appeared on the branch over the years. In 1957 Nos. 46284, 46287 and 46296 were working alongside former LSWR composites Nos. 5136 and 6529 and ex-LSWR thirds converted to seconds, Nos. 169 and 3039.

Between 1935 and 1936 a total of 133 ex-LSWR non-corridor coaches were rebuilt, many having extensive body alterations and all being mounted on new underframes. At least three of the rebuilds were allocated to Hayling Island branch services: lavatory third No. 169 between 1957 and 1959, brake third No. 2616 in 1957 and 1958 and composite No. 4753 from 1955 until 1958. The lavatory third No. 169, originally a 48 ft third and reintroduced into service in January 1931 to SR diagram 31, in its new guise seated 88 passengers. Brake third No. 2616 was formerly No. 4750 and was rebuilt in August 1936 to diagram 97 and seated 68 third class passengers, whilst composite No. 4753, formerly No. 4608 in its rebuilt state emerged in July 1939 to diagram 286 and seated 12 first and 60 third class passengers. All vehicles, originally 48 ft in length, were 61 ft 7 in. over buffers, had a body length of 58 ft, body width 8 ft 0¾ in., width over guard's ducket 9 ft 0 in., maximum height 11 ft 11 in., bogie wheelbase 8 ft 0 in. and bogie centres 40 ft 0 in. No. 169 was withdrawn in July 1959, No. 2616 in October 1959 and No. 4753 in November 1958.

By 1962 Maunsell SR corridor brake composites Nos. 6697 and 6699 of diagram 2403 and formerly in coach sets 618 and 619 respectively appeared on the branch as loose coaches often working together, sometimes supported by Bulleid-designed brake composite No. 6721. Nos. 6697 and 6699 had body length of 59 ft 0 in. and width of 9 ft 0 in. In the same year the only example of an all-fibreglass-bodied coach was built at Eastleigh works on the underframe of a coach destroyed in the 1957 Lewisham accident. The cost of conversion was totally uneconomic, but after trials as No. DS70200 it was numbered S1000S and worked on the Hayling Island branch throughout 1963 until closure of the line. The compartments of this vehicle featured three experimental styles of décor. After a long period in store at Micheldever, the

East Somerset Railway at Cranmore eventually acquired the vehicle in 1973. In the latter years examples of Bulleid-designed corridor stock infiltrated to the branch with examples of brake composite, composite and full third, later second class, loose vehicles added to the formation. These were of standard dimensions: length over buffers 67 ft 1 in., body length 64 ft 6 in., bodyside length 63 ft 6 in., length of underframe 63 ft 5 in., body width 9 ft 0 in., height from rail to roof centre 12 ft 4½ in., height from roof centre to top of periscope on brake vehicles 8⅜ in., bogie wheelbase 8 ft 0 in. and bogie centres 46 ft 6 in.

One of the reasons proffered for the closure of the branch was 'ageing stock' and whilst this might have been true as regards the motive power it was certainly not applicable to the coaching stock, which since 1957 had been relatively modern. Only Maunsell brake corridor composites No 6697 and 6699, dating from 1935, were scrapped in December 1963 as a result of the branch closure; the remaining coaches used on the line were allocated for use elsewhere on the Southern Region.

The livery of LBSCR coaching stock prior to 1870 was varnished for first and first/second composites, varnish or painted lake for saloons, second class were varnished or painted brown with some dark green, whilst thirds were painted brown or dark green. Starting in 1870 and until 1903 all coaching stock was varnished mahogany with gilt lining but later it was a paint finish. Roofs were white and the running gear black. From 1903 until 1911 the livery was umber and white with gilt lettering shaded blue and from 1911 until Grouping plain umber with gold shaded black lettering. The SR initially adopted the Maunsell sage/olive green livery for coaching stock and this was changed from 1937 to Malachite green. Both liveries included black ends and underframing. BR continued to use the SR green but then introduced for a short period a red or maroon livery before changing back to a slightly darker green.

Wagons

The wagons used by the Hayling Railway and during the early LBSCR era were wooden open vehicles with side doors and fitted with dumb buffers. Where grain, straw or merchandise were susceptible to wet weather, a tarpaulin sheet was utilized to cover the contents of the wagon. The brake van at the tail of the train would have been a 7½ ton vehicle. In the years prior to the turn of the century the LBSCR used three-plank 6 ton dropside open wagons to LBSCR class 'B' with wooden frames dating from 1896 for the conveyance of general merchandise and minerals. These measured 18 ft 5 in. over buffers, had a wheelbase of 9 ft 6 in. and height of 5 ft 9 in. These wagons were gradually superseded by four-plank 8 ton capacity opens to LBSCR class 'D', SR diagram 136, and measuring 18 ft 5 in. over buffers, a 9 ft 6 in. wheelbase and overall height of 7 ft 2 in. Later 10 ton five-plank opens with square and round ends to SR diagram 1371 with a length of 18 ft 5 in. over buffers, 9 ft 6 in. wheelbase and height of 8 ft 10 ½ in. were also used. Another variation was the use of 8 ton five-plank opens with bar LBSCR class 'A', later SR diagram 1370, measuring 18 ft 5 in. over buffers and 9 ft 6 in. wheelbase also a 10 ton five-plank open with bar also to SR diagram 1370 and measuring 18 ft 5 in. over buffers and with a 9 ft 3 in. wheelbase. Other open wagons included 10 ton five-plank to SR diagram 1369 with 18 ft 5 in. length over buffers, 9 ft 3 in. wheelbase and overall height of 9 ft 0¼ in.; 10 ton five-plank open with steel underframe, introduced from 1920, to SR diagram 1368 measuring 18 ft 5 in. over buffers, 9 ft 0 in. wheelbase and overall height of 8 ft 10¾ in.; 10 ton six-plank open to SR diagram 1372 measuring 18 ft 5 in, over buffers, 9 ft 6 in. wheelbase and overall height of 7 ft 7¾ in. Locomotive coal might have arrived in 12 ton seven-plank opens to SR diagram 1373 measuring 19 ft 6 in. over buffers 9 ft 0 in. wheelbase and overall height of 8 ft 3⅝ in. For fruit and perishable traffic 8 ton ventilated vans to diagram 1433 were provided, measuring 21 ft 4 in. over buffers, 9 ft 9 in. wheelbase and overall height of 11 ft 3 in. Later covered goods vans to SR diagram 1434 were also utilized. They measured 21 ft 4 in. over buffers, had a wheelbase of 9 ft 9 in. and were 11 ft 6 in. in height.

The small amount of cattle traffic conveyed to or from Hayling Island would have entailed the use of 6 tons capacity cattle wagons to SR diagram 1527 measuring 21 ft 4 in. over buffers with 11 ft 2 in. wheelbase and 11 ft 11 in. high. At the tail of the train a variety of brake vans would have been provided including Stroudley 7½ ton road brake to SR diagram 1564 measuring 19 ft 0 in. over buffers, 9 ft 9 in. wheelbase and overall height 10 ft 5 in. (11 ft 8 in. over chimney); 10 and 12 ton both to SR diagram 1568 measuring 16 ft 0 in. over buffers, 9 ft 9 in. wheelbase and height of 11 ft 7½ in. (12 ft 10 in. over chimney); and 15 ton capacity to SR diagram 1574 measuring 21 ft 0 in. over buffers, 10 ft 6 in. wheelbase and overall height of 11 ft 8 in. (12 ft 10¾ in. over chimney). For a number of years the allocated goods brake van for the branch was LBSCR No. 234, SR No. 55781 to SR diagram 1568 built in 1896 and allocated to work between Havant and Hayling Island only. It was withdrawn in May 1947. In addition many wagons owned by other railway companies were used to deliver and collect agricultural and livestock traffic, whilst coal and coke supplies came in private owner coal wagons. These fell into two categories, those belonging to the collieries consigning coal, and merchant and coal factor wagons, which were loaded at collieries.

After Grouping, the LBSCR wagons continued to be utilized and SECR and LSWR wagons soon infiltrated into the system. Gradually SR standard design wagons made an appearance. The most numerous were probably the 12 ton, eight-plank opens to diagram 1316, with a 10 ft 6 in. wheelbase, 18 ft 0 in. body length, 21 ft 0 in. over buffers, width of 7 ft 11 in. and height of 8 ft 9⅞ in. Another type was 12 ton, eight-plank open to diagram 1379, with 9 ft 0 in. wheelbase, measuring 17 ft 6 in. over headstocks, 20 ft 6 in. over buffers with a width of 7 ft 11 in. and height of 8 ft 7⅞ in. Yet another open used was 10 ton capacity five-plank to diagram 1380, with 9 ft 0 in. wheelbase, measuring 17 ft 6 in. over headstocks, 20 ft 6 in. over buffers and with a maximum width of 7 ft 11 in. Another variant was 12 ton, eight-plank open with 9 ft 0 in. wheelbase to diagram 1385. These measured 17 ft 6 in. over headstocks, 20 ft 6 in. over buffers, had a maximum width of 7 ft 11 in. and height of 8 ft 7⅞ in. Later variations included a 12 ton, eight-plank open wagon to diagram 1400, with 10 ft 0 in. wheelbase, measuring 17 ft 6 in. over headstocks, 20 ft 6 in. over buffers, maximum width of 7 ft 11 in. and height of 8 ft 7¾ in. Last came the 13 ton five-plank open to diagram 1375, with 10 ft 0 in. wheelbase, measuring 17 ft 6 in. over headstocks, 20 ft 6 in. over buffers, with a width of 8 ft 0 in. and maximum height of 7 ft 2⅞ in. All were used on vegetable and root crop traffic as well as coal and coke traffic.

Occasional use was made of the 12 ton capacity flat truck for containers to diagram 1382, with 9 ft 0 in. wheelbase, measuring 17 ft 6 in. over headstocks and 20 ft 11 in. over buffers. Fitted and unfitted 12 ton, 9 ft 0 in. wheelbase covered vans with equal planking to diagram 1428, conveyed perishable goods, fruit, and malt. These measured 17 ft 6 in. over headstocks and had a wheelbase of 20 ft 11 in. A second 12 ton capacity variant with unequal planking to diagram 1455, with a 10 ft 0 in. wheelbase was also used. These were 17 ft 6 in. over headstocks, 20 ft 6 in. over buffers and had a maximum height of 12 ft 2¹³⁄₁₆ in. The ever decreasing amount of cattle traffic would have arrived and departed in the early style of cattle wagon to diagram 1529 with 10 ft 6 in. wheelbase and measuring 19 ft 0 in. over headstocks, 22 ft 5 in. over buffers, with maximum width of 8 ft 4¾ in. and height of 11 ft 3¾ in. The later style to diagram 1530 had 10 ft 6 in. wheelbase and measured 19 ft 0 in. over headstocks, 22 ft 1 in. over buffers, 8 ft 4¾ in. wide and had a height of 11 ft 3¾ in. Agricultural machinery destined for local farms was delivered on former LBSCR 20 ton well wagons to SR diagram 1686 with 15 ft 0 in. wheelbase and overall length over headstocks of 20 ft 2 in. and measuring 23 ft 2 in. over buffers. After 1947 SR standard goods brake vans infiltrated the branch and consisted of three types: 25 ton capacity to diagram 1578 and 1579 both with 16 ft wheelbase and measuring 24 ft 0 in. over headstocks, 27 ft 0 in. over buffers with a maximum width of 8 ft 6 in. over the guard's ducket and height of 11 ft 5⅛ inches. The third type was of 15 tons capacity to diagram 1581 with similar dimensions but maximum height of 11 ft 1⅞ in. After nationalization many of the older wooden wagons were scrapped and much of the traffic was conveyed in the standard BR 16 ton all-steel mineral wagons.

In LBSCR days before 1895 the body, solebars and headstock of open wagons and vans were painted a very pale 'lavender grey' and instead of company name or initials identity was shown with a symbol of a white shield superimposed by a red cross, the whole being placed within a blue circle. The ironwork below solebar level, buffer guides, buffers, drawbars, drawbar plates and couplings was black. Brake vans carried the same livery but with the company initials, however the ends were painted a bright vermilion. In the period from 1895 to 1911 the basic body colour was altered to a darker shade of grey officially termed 'lead' colour, ironwork was black and roofs of vans and brake vans white. The vermilion painting of the ends of brake vans ceased in 1904. From 1911 the grey base colour of bodywork on the wagons was darkened and from thereon the letters 'LBSC' were applied to the sides. The SR wagon livery continued the tradition of the LSWR of dark brown with white lettering, with the brake vans painted the same save that the headstocks, veranda ends and inner body ends were painted Venetian red. BR livery was grey for non-fitted vehicles and bauxite for all fitted stock.

The following service vehicles were prohibited from the Hayling Island branch due to axle weight restrictions.

Diagram	Vehicle
471	30 ton bogie bolster wagon
572	20 ton sleeper and ballast wagons (Grampus)
583	20 ton hopper ballast wagon (Mackerel)
642	50 ton bogie rail wagon (Salmon)
—	50 ton bogie rail sleeper and ballast utility wagon (Sturgeon)
SR 1598	Borail wagon (permitted to run over the line provided load did not exceed 20 tons uniformly distributed)
SR 1735	Hopper

In the event of a defect to coaching stock or wagons the carriage and wagon examiner at Havant was delegated to attend but early in SR days the position was withdrawn and thereafter the examiner travelled from Portsmouth & Southsea to attend to the offending vehicle.

Level Crossings

No.	Location	Mileage m.	ch.	Local name	Status
	Havant station	0	00		
1	Havant & Langston	0	09	New Lane	Public Road
2	Havant & Langston	0	71	Wade Court	Footpath
3	Havant & Langston	1	06	Langston Farm	Occupation
4	Havant & Langston	1	07	Langston	Public Road
	Langston	1	09		
5	Langston & North Hayling	1	13	Langston Mill	Occupation
6	Langston & North Hayling	1	66	Causeway	Footpath
7	North Hayling & Hayling Island	2	09	Oyster Creek	Occupation
	North Hayling	2	35		
8	North Hayling & Hayling Island	2	36¼	North Hayling	Footpath
9	North Hayling & Hayling Island	2	71½	Knott's Marsh	Occupation
10	North Hayling & Hayling Island	3	11¼	West Stoke	Occupation
11	North Hayling & Hayling Island	4	03	Sinah Creek	Occupation
12	North Hayling & Hayling Island	4	18½	Sinah Lake	Occupation
	Hayling Island	4	45		

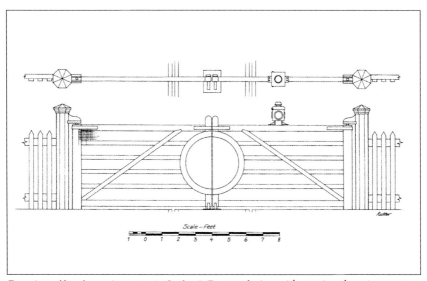

Drawing of level crossing gates to Saxby & Farmer design with cast-iron hanging posts at New Lane level crossing Havant.

Appendix Two

Bridges

No.	Location	Mileage m. ch.	Local name	Under or over	Type	Spans No.	Square span between abutments or supports ft in.	Depth of construction ft in.	Distance from road or surface of water to rail ft in.	Construction
1	Havant & Langston	00 25½	East Street	Over	Public road	1	15 6	3 2	16 0	Brick abutments, brick arch and parapets
2	Havant & Langston	00 32½	Town Hall	Over	Public footbridge	1	55 6	0 9	14 3	Wrought iron lattice and timber
2A	Havant & Langston	00 48	Havant Bypass	Over	Public	1				Brick and concrete (proposed)
3	Langston & North Hayling	01 49	Langston viaduct	Under	River	25	19 0 each	1 6	10 0*	Timber
						1	50 0			50 ft opening span
										30 ft clearance for shipping.
									23 0†	Wrought iron centre span
										Width of structure 14 ft 6 in.
						25	19 0 each			Timber

There were no skew spans between abutments or supports on the above bridges.

* Above high water mark.   † Above low water mark.

Acknowledgements

The publication of this history would not have been possible without the help of many people who have been kind enough to assist in whatever way they could. In particular I should like to thank the National Archives, British Railways Southern Region, The Hampshire County Record Office, House of Lords Record Office, British Library Newspaper Library, Transport Users' Consultative Committee and the National Railway Museum, also active and retired railway staff of the Southern Region, some of whom worked on the Hayling Island branch and members of the LBSCR Circle. The late R.C. (Dick) Riley provided additional notes on several subjects after reading through the original manuscript, Doug Stevenson, Brian Jackson and David Gould provided useful information, Michael Back and Chris Cock confirmed some signalling details and Robert Powell kindly checked the revised work.

Bibliography

General Works
Regional History of Railways of Great Britain Volume II (David & Charles)
London Brighton and South Coast Railway, C. Hamilton Ellis (Ian Allan)
Rails in the Isle of Wight, Allen and McLeod (Allen & Unwin)
Isle of Wight Railways, R.M. Robbins (Oakwood Press)
The Portsmouth-Ryde Passage, Mackett (Ravensbourne Press)
Locomotives of the London Brighton and South Coast Railway, D.L. Bradley (RCTS)
Bogie Carriages of the LBSCR, David Gould (Oakwood Press)
Maunsell's SR Steam Carriage Stock, David Gould (Oakwood Press)
Bulleid's SR Steam Passenger Stock, David Gould (Oakwood Press)
LSWR Carriages, Volume I, G.R. Weddell (Wild Swan)

Periodicals
Bradshaw's Railway Guides
Bradshaw's Railway Timetables
British Railways (Southern Region) Magazine
Buses
Herapath's Journal
Illustrated London News
Naval Chronicle
Railway Magazine
Railway Times
Railway World
Southern Railway Magazine
Trains Illustrated

Newspapers
Hampshire Post
Hampshire Telegraph
Isle of Wight County Press
Isle of Wight Times
Portsmouth Times
The Times

Also
Minute Books – Hayling Railway, LBSCR and Southern Railway
Working Timetables – LBSCR, Southern Railway and BR (SR)
Appendices to Working Timetables – LBSCR, SR and BR (SR)
Public Timetables – LBSCR, SR and BR (SR)

Index